Elegant Rage
A Poetic Tribute to Woody Guthrie

Dorothy Alexander, Editor

Copyright © 2012
Village Books Press

First Edition, First Printing, June 2012

Cover Art: Bert Seabourn

Village Books Press
Cheyenne, Oklahoma

ISBN: 978-1-936923-03-8

Introduction

Woody Guthrie was born July 14, 1912 in Okemah, Oklahoma and reared in Oklahoma. He was a champion of the disenfranchised, minorities and the working class, a colorful and beloved folk hero. He was part of a primitive tradition, carried through the ages by common people to express their joy and anger and frustrations through music. Their drudgery and occasional triumphs. Their intense independence.

This volume of poetry is a tribute to Woody Guthrie, who on the 100th anniversary of his birth, remains one of the patron saints of American rebelliousness, still causing trouble posthumously, inspiring generation after generation of singer-songwriters-poets, and all those who feel constrained by conformity. Joe Klein, one of his biographers, says he was struck by Woody's *"elegant rage."*

It is the hope and the goal of the poets whose work is collected here to memorialize the history and culture of common people everywhere. To raise world consciousness of the present-day struggles of the working class and all those who are oppressed by the current brand of "fascists.' To voice an *elegant rage* at the social and political injustice of this 21st Century, as Woody Guthrie would if he still walked the highways of this country today.

Dorothy Alexander, Editor

Dorothy Alexander, Editor

Dorothy Alexander has coordinated the poetry readings at the annual Woody Guthrie Folk Festival in Okemah and in Oklahoma City for the past three years. She, along with her partner, Devey Napier, and Village Books Press, sponsor the ongoing First Sunday Poetry Readings at Beans and Leaves in Oklahoma City. She plans a series of readings throughout 2012 celebrating Woody Guthrie's Centennial.

Bert Seabourn, Cover Artist

Bert Seabourn, primarily a painter of Indian subjects, is an American expressionist who also paints non-Indian figures, landscapes, and occasionally flowers. As an expressionist, he uses the technique of dripping, smearing, and splattering the paint--acrylic, oil and watercolor. He also works with graphics. In 1976, the Five Civilized Tribes of Oklahoma designated Seabourn a Master Artist.

The editor and the poets whose work is featured here are deeply grateful for Bert's generosity in providing the art appearing on the cover of this volume of poetry dedicated to the art of Woody Guthrie on the centennial of his birth.

Table of Contents

Abigail Keegan teaches British and Women's Literature at Oklahoma City University. She has authored a critical book on Lord Byron's Oriental Tales. Her poetry books include *The Feast of the Assumptions, Oklahoma Journey* and *Depending on the Weather*, published by Village Books Press, and selected as a finalist for the 2012 Oklahoma Book Award. She is currently working on two new collections of poetry, *Road Work* and *Hearing Voices*.

Road Work

Driving to Arkansas sand piled
mountains rise, trees lay down
their lives for us. Concrete
trucks turn and churn
white lava, earth movers,
and miles of men unfurl
America's pathways through
Arkansas, Oklahoma, Texas
Mississippi and Tennessee
everywhere I've been
high and low ways,
bridges and byways cross
and new worlds unfold here
from where we've been and
where we will be as workers
carve another face into America.

Gay Marriage, 1995

When we were in Arkansas,
a cottage garden grew like
wild flowers up to the door,
down the hill to evergreen hedge
where a cotton tail rabbit sheltered
himself in the shelf of a stone ledge,
and we held hands on a swing amid
bee-sweet music and soft wind
humming an ode to joy as the thick
August heat relaxed and lay back
under a large sweet gum trees,
light pink crepe myrtle confettied
all the world about us
as we promised our bodies
to honor, our goods to share,
our vows to come from the separate
poetry of selves into another song,
no minister, no crowd looked on
to bless or to deny
our forsaking of all others,
only we, the rabbit and bees
under gentle shade trees
were there that day,
and years ago with words to say
there is love
and the many choices we make
to draw on life and
draw our lives together.

Alan Berecka has published poetry in such places as *The Christian Century, Concho River Review,* and *Ruminate.* His latest collection of poems *Remembering the Body* was published in 2011 by Mongrel Empire Press. He is a librarian in Corpus Christi at Del Mar College and lives in Sinton, Texas.

The Way it Is

I keep having this dream. I'm sitting
in the balcony of an old movie house,
watching *It's a Wonderful Life* in 3-D
while chewing on salty and stale pop corn
that I can't wash down with a jumbo cup
of warm flat coke. The corn coheres into a gum
that I tongue and begin to blow into bubbles,
large bubbles as big as my head until one
explodes, covers my face in a gummy goo,
blinding my red and blue cardboard glasses,
so I take them off and try to scrape the lenses
clean. In the pale glow of blue light
bouncing off the screen, I look around
and notice everyone else in the crowd
is wearing *Win one for the Gipper* buttons.
On the blurred screen, the film reaches
the part where the kindly Uncle Billy
taunts Mr. Potter (or is that Dick Cheney,
but no matter) and hands him by mistake
the Bailey's Building and Loan's deposit
which spells his nephew George's doom
and the crowd goes crazy and bursts
into a wild applause. I can't wake up.

Taxed

Long ago they mined the gold
but they didn't fill the potholes
that were left in all of our streets.
If it'll repave'em, raise my taxes, please.

Under the bridge there ain't no troll
just voodoo economics taking a toll
on the foreclosed-on American family.
If it'll bail'em out, raise my taxes, please.

Kids taking classes at the university
piling up the bills for tuition and fees.
They won't ever live a life debt free.
If it'll give'em aid, raise my taxes, please.

Where the teacher stood there's just a desk
with a bubble reading information kiosk
that'll turn our kids into test taking machines.
If it'll save creativity, raise my taxes, please.

Coming home from a party drunk on tea
some patriot wrapped his car around a tree.
Too bad the town can't pay cops or E.M.T.s.
If it'll save even him, raise my taxes, please.
No insurance, then it's on your knees.
Pray to be saved from preventable disease
or better yet make a home overseas.
If it'll cure us, raise my taxes, please.

Folks, look around and don't fight it.
Remember, we are one people united.
A buck spent on you, is a buck spent on me.
Let's help each other out. Raise our taxes please.

An Old Man Looks at Leadership

If it is the wise man who knows
what he does not know, then what
to make of the cocksure who yells,
Follow me! The Donner Party
had its leader, as did the Lost
Squadron, The Light Brigade
and Pickett's Charge. The Titanic
had its captain. General Custer
and Charlie Manson had pizzazz.

Even the greats had their faults.
Somewhere near the back of the pack
of the foot sore wandering Jews
some blue beard was muttering,
Oy, Moses the putz, like packing
a compass or better yet a map
would have been too much to ask?

The older I get the wearier
I become of leaders. Give me
a keeper, someone comfortable
in his ignorance who knows
that newer is not always better,
and I will gladly follow him
to my cage and lick his hand
as he turns the key in the lock.

Alan Gann, member of the Dallas Poets Community, is editor of the literary journal, Illya's Honey. He has poetry in Sentence, Main Street Rag, Borderlands, and North Texas Review. In 2011, he was nominated for a Pushcart Prize by Red River Review and a Best of the Net award by Red Fez. He teaches in the Dallas area and facilitates writing workshops.

When Ani Came to Town

We consider ourselves a liberal bunch
but nobody ever dropped an F-bomb
in the sanctuary of Green Meadows United Methodist Church
at least not from the stage, beneath the cross
into a microphone with all the church ladies present—
much less said the S- A- and P-words—
yes the P-word, said how much she loved to rub her own.

Now, the Outreach Committee had endorsed
the youth ministers plan to have folk music on Saturday Nights,
give the kids someplace to hangout, and everybody
grooved on the funny guy who sang environmental songs
and the lesbians who sang earnest, gender-neutral love songs
while making goo-goo eyes at one another got two encores

Then Ani came to play
and when she let the first one fly
we all looked to Nana Rose—saw her jaw clench,
thought she might get up and leave,
but then Ani launched into an old union song
and Nana started singing along.
And all night, that's the way it went—Bam!
followed by a sarcastic remark about the president
and we'd all laugh, almost relaxed,
waiting to see what happened next.

C. Alifair Skebe has published two books of poetry and
her work has appeared in national poetry and literary journals.
She lives in Albany, NY with her cheesemonger husband and
three children and teaches at the University of New York at
Albany.

A White Cast Iron Bathtub

White porcelain knobs reading *HOT* and *COLD*,
brushed nickel faucet, a warm stream, foaming bubbles,
soft music – you know the story –
Those soap commercials from the nineteen eighties
made baths a genre – a necessity –
like Frisbee in the park with the dog
or yoga meditation – or shopping –
Wondrously cleanse away the anxiety,
all the bad things from your life,
while the politicians are meeting,
the bankers are meeting,
the businessmen are meeting,
and all the housewives and nannies and teens and babies
and working moms recline singularly in little overfull tubs,
their round little knees peaking from the cloud-like foam,
their gentle, flowing locks pulled into a bun as wet ringlets
cascade down their bare white shoulders,
into white water rafting waterfalls and urban wilderness,
relaxing baths to a fantasy of whiteness –
bath salts and sea salts and essential oils
alchemically combine in a suburban-influenced stew
to make life better, happy, more tolerable,
until the warm bath itself becomes anxiety-provoking too,
because it is never quite enough and nothing ever seems to
wash away.

Ann Howells is on the board of Dallas Poets Communityand has edited their journal, *Illya's Honey,* for thirteen years. Her chapbook, *Black Crow in Flight*, was published by Main Street Rag. Nominated twice for Pushcart, once for Best of the Web, her work has appeared in *Borderlands, Calyx, River Sedge, and San Pedro River Review.*

Progress Comes

At the public end of a rough dirt road
mid bramble and Queen Anne's Lace,
he hand-lettered sign haphazardly askew.
CRAB POTS, it read. Watermen lived
in frame cottages; tall pines lined the shore.
Sounds of lumbering workboats echoed,
one-cylinder inboard engines, sunrise
through suppertime. Oysters tonged.
Seine nets hauled. Cork-floated trot lines
checked daily, crabs sold at wharves
where women cleaned and picked meat.
Long hours at minimum wage until
arthritis took their hands, cataracts
took their eyes. But recently, DC
discovered the lower county, one hour
south. Million dollar *cottages* crowd
shorelines, pools installed within sight
of the beach, sailboats and cabin cruisers
on the water for *fishing parties* and
oyster roasts. Floats bob near
unweathered piers: fresh crab for
weekenders. Macy's invaded Main Street;
superstores opened at crossroads;
BMWs appeared in parking lots; Perrier
on grocery shelves. Republicans made

a showing in last year's election. And
beside the road, a big, white sign:
CRUSTACEAN ENTRAPMENT DEVICES.
Not a one of them can call a pot, a pot.

Miss Nora

Lands, Chile, she'd say, *com'on over here*
an' lemme lookit you. You've growed some,
'deed, you have. Then, she'd gather me in a hug.
Miss Nora raised Daddy and Uncle Birch
after their Mama died, raised her own kids, too,
and three grandkids. Her house sat out on Hell's Point,
painted white with red trim and a white picket fence.
Her kitchen was red and white, too, center of her home,
parlor closed up except when the preacher came to call
smelled fusty—lemon oil and dust and stale tobacco.
But, the kitchen wafted cinnamon, yeast bread, chocolate—
sugar and spice and everything nice—as Miss Nora baked
loaves, biscuits, tall chocolate cakes and tangy lemon pies
topped with meringue light as spume on an incoming tide.
There was always something delicious cooling on the sill,
leading visitors by the nose, back toward the kitchen.
And after a tall glass of sweet iced tea with fresh mint,
and a big wedge of pie or thick slice of bread
slathered with real butter, we'd move to the porch to chat:
Miss Nora in her favorite rocking chair, fingers flashing
as she crocheted little jackets and caps for someone's
new baby, never glancing at her work, and never missing
either a stitch or snippet of conversation as her husband
grumbled about all she gave away. Her heart stopped
in her ninetieth year, as she was frosting a Baltimore cake.
If her spirit hovered near, she was probably saying,
Don't you let that cake set now! Frost it right quick;
run it down t' church 'fore the bake sale.

Family Photo

They pose together—five of them—
with the big, white rocking horse. Four
ride its back in various animated poses:
three brothers, one sister. Gin, the eldest,
stands beside. Line and angle. Flat chest.
No hips. Lank hair. Her clothes hang.
She does not want to be there. Notice
the background coop and chicken yard.
Her job: stand at a rough table adjoining
the fence, pump water and wipe shit
from eggs before packing them for market.
She hates it.

Classmates pass along the rutted road
and say hello. She looks through them,
does not respond, though her cheeks
blaze red.

Arn Henderson is an architect and Professor Emeritus of Architecture at OU. He has authored two books of poetry, *Document for an Anonymous Indian* and *The Surgeon General's Collection.* He also co-edited The Point Riders Great Plains Poetry Anthology and his work has appeared in several journals including World Literature Today, Nimrod, Interstate, Southwestern American Literature, Renegade 10, Broomweed Journal, Blood and Thunder and Cross Timbers.

Township 12 North Range 4 West

                    At the Stockyards
Caballero pushing cattle through the alley
                        to the loading pen's beckoning
chute
 Whistling with his fingers
                            to the counterpoint of a bawling
chorus
                    such elegant and pitiful sounds
                    on the day of Sacrifice
                            beat   the   base   drum
slowly
                    Measure   by   Measure

Township 1 South Range 16 East

Passing
            bales of straw
                                    yellow and stacked
                    black starlings picking
Passing
            over creek thick with cottonwoods
                        sighing
                                in the wind

                    heavy
                                        with years
                    thick
                                        of shadows
            in the lace of reflections
Passing
                nests of red cedar
                        scented
                                            with a poisonous broth
                    brown as a mummy
                                        woven
            with grey humps of Brahma cows
            in a tapestry
                        of the Meridian

Cimarron Base Line

Listening to the black dog breathe
                            sleeping at my side
            Silk and shining black under the touch of my
                                                stroke
                        rising and falling of torso as I lean into the
wheel of night
                                whispering of dreams
            Traveling man on the move
dog and I

Audrey Streetman's poems have appeared in Oklahoma Today, Blood & Thunder, Crosstimbers, ByLine Magazine, New Plains Review, Poet Magazine, Potpourri, Pegasus and Voices International. She has published three chapbooks, *The Train*, *A Gathering of Bones*, *Keeper of the Dream* and a memoir, *The Well*. Audrey is a graduate of Durham Business College, the University of Central Oklahoma, and University of Oklahoma Commercial Lending School. She is retired and writes full time.

Through the Window of a Laundromat

A woman folds clothes in neat stacks.
On her face lines deep with sorrow
or wisdom. She speaks to a child
who lays her doll aside, begins
to take clothes from the dryer. I think

it must be hot because the woman takes a cloth
from the counter, wipes sweat from her face.
I wonder if she is legal, if she has a husband,
rents a house, owns a car. I want to speak
to her, but I tell myself my Spanish is poor
and I walk away.

Barbara Shepherd has won numerous awards, including the 2012 Oklahoma Writers Federation Lifetime Achievement Award for writing and painting, is a Woody Guthrie Poet, an Oklahoma Poet Laureate Nominee, a Lone Stars Poet, and was twice-named ACW's Writer of the Year. She has been published in books and journals and sponsors the Annual Art Affair Writing Contest.

Dusty Bowls

An Oklahoma family sat in silence
inside their closed farmhouse,
July's air humid and heavy,
thick as cold grits.

Through windows, fastened tight,
seams stuffed with rags,
they watched tumbleweeds skate by.
Red dirt swirled.

Little girls set the table,
turned plates and bowls upside down,
and helped bring food from the kitchen.

The father prayed for the wind to stop,
for soil to rest again on the ground.
When they opened their eyes,
they saw dirt had filtered in,
leaving a fine coat of dust on their old china.
Wash Monday

Morning began like any Monday
without rain.
An Oklahoma family prayed for relief
from drought in the southern plains,

did the wash,
hung clothes outside on a line.

Surprised to see a dark cloud
appear on the horizon,
they hoped it would bring rain by noon
and left the clothes to finish drying.

But, the cloud moved fast,
covering the whole sky,
choking out the sunlight.
No funnels formed. No sprinkles came.
But the noise – an insidious roar.

The parents herded their children inside,
closed up the house and watched huge insects
bang against windows.

Locusts ate everything green,
devoured tree leaves, crops and flowers,
left plant stalks only if they were brown.

Swarms attacked the wash on the clothesline.
Green and white gathered skirts
hung in shreds after giant grasshoppers
stripped them of their emerald stripes.
Locusts chewed sap green leaves and vines
from embroidered dresser scarves and chomped
viridian lace edgings crocheted on towels.

The pests left as quickly as they had come.

Barrie Neller was born in London in 1932, served in the Royal Irish Fusiliers and emigrated to Canada in 1956. He moved to New York and later to Dallas, Texas. After retiring from the advertising business, he began writing poetry. His work is published in Red River Review and Illya's Honey, a chapbook and three anthologies. He is a member of the Dallas Poetry Community and WordSpace.

Oklahoma Bombing Anniversary

Like a one-eyed giant awakening,
the sun delivers the dawn
then helps us shake the
chill of slumber.
Squeaking like bed springs,
the birds spread the news
of a new day.
Recognizing the date, our dream machines
re-program themselves and recall
the sorrowful horror.
And to protect us through the day
poetry takes shape in our heads.
Reflected images take over
our imagination.
Minds are busy with fresh
descriptions of details already described.
So common man, woman and child
can be commemorated
by uncommon language
from unlikely sources.

Benjamin Myers' latest book is *Lapse Americana* (forthcoming from New York Quarterly Books). He won the Oklahoma Book Award for his first book, *Elegy for Trains*. His poems appear in *Nimrod, DMQ, Borderlands, Tar River Poetry, The New York Quarterly, Plainsongs, The Iron Horse Literary Review*, and many others."

Summer Work

There is a sky like sharpened bone
over the trailer home
with tinfoil in all the windows,
where I wait while my foreman
smokes weed from a metal pipe.

We were to start early –
already it's hot –
but I had to pick him up
again. He won't go
until he's high. Outside
beneath the mangy
mimosa over the dirt
drive, a dog on a chain
whines against the heat
loudly enough to be heard
inside above the box fan.

The big boss will have finished
with the bobcat and is waiting
for our shovels to even the dig,
where the concrete will be poured,
where the pool will be lined
with cool blue plastic, behind
the house we never go into.

My foreman is a screw-up
named Joe, with a suspended
license, a trailer on the margins,
and a married girlfriend
who smokes like a damp log.

He is sitting on the spotted brown carpet,
leaning back against a couch,
pipe in one hand, lighter in the other,
and he's telling me about his first
year out of high school – expelled,
not graduated – how he'd actually get
up early, since he didn't have to,
and walk off into the aimless housing
of Edmond, Oklahoma in the 70's. He's taking
 a drag and staring at the wall. He's telling
me how he would steal motorcycles,

how he would move through the early dark,
trying each garage door with his fingers
until he felt one give. He's telling me
how he would raise it just
enough and crawl beneath
on his belly. He's remembering
how the concrete always felt warm,
how his eyes would adjust in the dark
garage, how if there was no bike
he would crawl back out, how if there was

he would hotwire it quick as cussing,
throw the door up, and burn
off down the street. He's telling me how
he would spend the day just riding
and riding, finally humming out along the lake
shore, the vast and manmade reservoir
beyond the city limits. He's telling me

how he'd walk the bike along the frail
rail bridge, rubber tires rubbing over wooden
slats, to a gap in the rusty trellis, how
he'd push the bike over the edge, the headlamp
on so he could watch the circle of light
sink into the murk below

The Drought

Long down the throat of hot
drought, the farmer sits
at his kitchen table and runs
nervous fingers through
gray hair, a herd
of deer running
through scant wood.

Nothing falling for weeks,
the man drags his pencil over
the furrows of his figures,
a cup of tepid coffee at his elbow.

His wife is at the sink.
Each time she moves by
he can smell the rain.

Bertha Wise is a Professor of English at Oklahoma City Community College. Her poetry has been published in various college anthologies—*Baraza* (at UCO), *Redbud* (at OSU-OKC), *Pegasus* (at Rose State College), *Salt River Anthology* (at Northern Oklahoma College), and *Absolute* (at OCCC).

Out of Context

I had a growing
realization that we
were out of
context with
the rest of the world—

that as we looked through
our microscopes and
telescopes and sometimes
even kaleidoscopes
the images were out of
kilter
lacking all the right
conditions to see
things right before our eyes—

we watched missiles firing
we listened for the last hurrah
we waited to be briefed by
someone who could put it all
into perspective—

but over time
you stuck to your belief
that knowing is in the detail of
what you saw smeared on a slide—

that you knew what you
viewed in the heavens
could be created by only One—
and the crystalline colors forming patterns
were ever changing—

through it all you
made us sensitive to the knowledge
that even learning out of context
would eventually connect
us to each other.

Carl Wade Thompson is a college English professor
and student currently working on his Ph.D. His pursuits
include writing poetry and short fiction of his native
Southeastern Oklahoma home, celebrating the rural lifestyle
he grew up in and learning more about small town culture.

The Shoe Salesman

This was the first job he had
Where he wore a white collar.
Didn't bother him that he sold shoes,
Measured feet all day.
It was nice to get off at five,
Instead of digging ditches.
Sometimes, as he fitted someone with his tender touch,
He wondered what they thought of him.
Would they see him the same, if they knew
That he had invaded Normandy,
The last survivor of his squad on Omaha beach?
He saw his friends cut down by a lead rain
And prayed to God he would last the day.
Had drove all over the United States,
Seen places others could only dream of?
Would they even know he could keep a Ford running,
With only spit and bailing wire?
No, they wouldn't know.
Probably don't even care.
"Do you have my size?" A customer asks.
As a good salesman he answers
"Sure."

A Meat Packer's Lament

My hands hurt.
They always do nowadays.
Wrinkled, worn, calloused,
a thousand days spent freezing,
packing meat piece by piece,
blood stained apron frigid,
clinging like a sheath.
I can always see my breath,
dragon smoke rising,
could have cut it with a knife.
Mental ventilation clanging nonstop,
ears ringing all the time now.
Can't hear silence anymore,
don't know what it feels like.
All I hear is machines,
Feel the meat locker around me.
How I wish for blue skies,
summer winds touching me.
But when I get out it's always night,
only the stars keep me company.

Carol Hamilton has recent publications in White Wall Review, Poet Lore, South Carolina Review, Cold Mountain Review, Tulane Review, Slipstream, Tar River Review, San Pedro River Review, California Quarterly, Us Newsetter, Poem, Flint Hills Review, and others. Recent books are Lexicography, March Street Press, and Master Of Theater: Peter The Great, Finishing Line Press. She is a former Poet Laureate of Oklahoma.

No Hard Travelin'

Oklahoma is fluffed up with moisture
and the sky is not huge this year,
so fringed with green and soft sway of edges.
Still, we commemorate those hard days
when bellies were as flat as the horizons
and the music had an ironic twang.
All was tight-strung and lean then.
Everything was moving out,
even the dirt itself.
We still talk a little tough
though the life is soft and hazy.
We wait till darkness breathes thick
and humid to go outside awhile.
We like to think we've seen it all,
but in the plain talk of that day,
"We ain't seen nothin'."

Tent Revivals

The hot world smeared past
as it does when we drive and talk.
Beside me she said she was
too afraid of doing wrong
to ever sneak into one as we did.
Our young world was made of dare devil
challenge and do. Those hot-breathed
summer nights when the prairie
exhaled its pent up portion
of sun fire's battering,
we would sneak in the back,
giggling. We sat on metal folding chairs,
snickered at the rolling and railing,
at the preacher, wild-eyed, pacing, shouting,
tossing hymnbooks and lecterns
off the platform made of raw-wood planks.
Street sounds of passing tires on concrete
and yellow porch lights across the way
sunk down in the mire of sin and fear.
Our giggles were nervous.
We never stayed long.
The sweat of the penitents overpowered
the scent of the baked prairie grasses.
My friend stayed away from fear,
and we feared to stay in that space
of stifling sureness. We slunk
away into our vast landscape,
telling and re-telling the tale.
We laughed with our happy lost souls.

Carol Davis Koss, A New Yorker by birth, has lived in Oklahoma City for over 40 years. She taught English, Creative Writing, and Remedial Reading from middle school through college. She is the author of *Chapter and Verse* (1997), *Camera Obscura* (2001 Oklahoma Book Award finalist), and *Painted Full of Tongues* (2002). Her poetry has appeared in numerous publications. She graduated from City College of New York and Purdue University.

The Scar Seemed Fresh

The scar seemed fresh – new, not bleeding; but he was sure there had been blood – maybe last night or this morning. It was a Wednesday in November, and he was in his corner booth at the diner. Snow was promised, but – as yet – only gray smudges gathered in the evening sky.

He noticed the scar, more than a bruise, when she brought the coffee she knew he'd want. It started on the back of her hand near the pinky and ran, almost serrated, to her wrist. He kept his attention on the coffee. Then, on her eyes as he ordered this Wednesday's special – catfish, a side of slaw, a twice-baked potato.

He tried to catch her eyes, but they were focused past the window, toward the first flurries caught in the streetlight, threaded through the beginnings of night. Last week, there'd been a bruise on her cheek. A month ago – a cut on her lip.

The catfish was deep-fried, crisp. The slaw – undistinguished by anything except too much mayonnaise. He put butter and sour cream on the potato. As he ate, she wiped down the table in the booth next to his. The smell of disinfectant spray mingled with catfish and burgers.

At the counter she was refilling salt and peppershakers, and sugar bowls, when a couple entered and took the clean booth next to his. They'd been there a few other Wednesdays, but were new enough to the diner and each other – to be careful with gestures, still learning what each would order, how each plied fork and knife and the space between their words – still needing menus. New enough not to know that soup, burgers, and the specials were their best bets.

They ordered steaks and fries. She wanted hers medium rare – he – very rare on the inside. He was tempted to lean over and tell them both would arrive well-done, but said nothing, and settled for noticing the flurries had stopped – the air grown still – and a thin moon – barely outlined by dark.

An hour until closing. He drank another cup of coffee, pulled a newspaper from his coat pocket and turned to the crossword puzzle.

She brought the steaks and the couple stared at her hand, Which she left visible longer than he thought necessary or prudent.

Three more people arrived, sat at the counter. A low throb of conversation – the dishwasher behind the swinging kitchen doors – an ambulance siren somewhere not too close.

Closing time. He'd finished the puzzle and returned the newspaper to his coat pocket. She removed her apron. They left together.

Catherine "Katey" Johnson, aka KariGrant performs standup comedy coast to coast, painted a twenty-foot mural (Continental Building—OKC), has photography in the IPHF's permanent collection; exhibited twice at NCHF&WHM and won National Awards in art and poetry. She is published in textbooks, anthologies and literary journals, won International awards for scripts, written and produced for cable and AOL. She loves her children, grandchildren, dear friends, pets, and the creative process.

Old Is Fast

You got a new car
Hood full of horses
Face jammed against your skull
When pedal meets plush pile.
But that's slo-mo, friend
'cause old comes at-cha fast.

It slams you into a brick wall
Two-thirty in the morning
You're about to wet the bed
So, you hurry to the bathroom
Man that's a trip
'cause the five meds they got you on
Give you the Tilt-a-Whirl dizzies,
But you gotta' get there *fast*!
And you do--
Whirling lightning--
That's you
Old real fast.

Dancing at the Prom yesterday
Now you're stirring

Fiber in your juice
Coughed up a piece of lung
Before toes hit floor.

At the Casino, you realize
Your insurance is a gamble, too
You're betting you'll die,
Become dismembered, or worse.
How the hell do you win that bet
That bet against the temple?
And that stupid chin hair
Comes back every thirty-minutes
Jewelry box replaced
With old people trinkets
Thermometer, BP cuff, hearing-aid,
Moleskin toe pads,
Corn removers, wart-off,
Magnifying glass, Gel pads,
Icy-Hot patches, things to make you go,
Things to make you stop,
Medicated pads,
Pads to catch the drips, flashlight,
Tweezers for that damn chin hair.
All of it piles high overnight
Cause old happens fast.

Your Mr. T starter kit
All says "Medic Alert"
Diabetic,
Pacemaker,
Allergic to Ibuprofen,
Percoset,
Darvon,
Penicillin,
Laytex,
And Cherries;

On Aspirin,
On Norvasc,
On HCL, Zoloft,
On Glucophage, on Niaspan,
On Donner and Blitzen,
Shit, what was I saying?
Oh, yeah, old is fast.

Titanium frames your blind eyes
Binds your bones together.
Blood pressure's up, pulse is down
So the Pacemaker zaps you forty-four percent
Of every twenty-four/seven.
You went in for a sleep test
When sex probably would have fixed it
And came out with a Zippo sized lump
Above your left tit
That happened fast.

Is that Raquel Welch on CSI?
Damn, I hope I look that good at seventy-one.
All I know is
It'll be here in a minute.

And him over there, not any better,
His arteries get real hard
If only he could use his arteries to--
He sets the TV tray aside to go get the mail
Knees knocking into his man apples,

We're old and we got here *fast.*

Charlie Rossiter, is a NEA Fellowship recipient and four-time Pushcart Prize nominee. He hosts the audio website poetrypoetry.com. He is the author of four books of poetry and numerous chapbooks. His work has been featured on NPR, and he was among the featured poets at the Oklahoma Laborfest in 2010. He lives near Chicago.

In the Wind

thirty degrees December morning
sun not yet up
over the White House
on the edge of Lafayette Park
shifting foot to foot--shoeless
surrounded by posters for peace
he stood on a wooden patform
in only a pair of ragged cut-off levis

there were goosebumps
on his chocolate skin
bare-chested
I said he was
cold wind blowing his foot long
    silver dreadlocks
he was   easy to see
cold
but he was smiling

surrounded by posters for peace
and looking like that,
some small-minded journalist
might be tempted
to make a geek
of the week story out of him,

but he was not a nut
he was undressed like that
he told us
because there'd be less hunger
and more peace in the world
if we'd all learn
to get along with less
that's what he said
standing on his wooden platform
barefoot, bare-chested
thirty degrees
long silver dreadlocks
blowing in the early morning wind.

(for Elijah Alfred Alexander, Jr. and for Concepcion Piccioto
who began the round-the-clock vigil for peace with special
emphasis on abolishment of nuclear weapons on June 3, 1981
and as of Fall 2011 was still there.)

Blues for Then
(after Rexroth)

Ah, to be young again
working a senseless job
for piss wages
all day sweating
under a sullen boss's
watchful eye
knowing that after dark
I'd be swimming naked
with you in the lake,
swimming inside you
on the moonlit beach,
blanketed only
by the star-filled sky.

Christine Wenk-Harrison lives in the Texas Hill Country where she writes a local food column for an online newspaper. She enjoys writing haiku and poems about nature, food and travel.

Journey to Big Bend

The Dustbowl Troubadour
ventured from Oklahoma to Texas,
traveling in a Model T,
first to the Panhandle, then Big Bend,
searching for buried treasure.

a road trip cloaked in legend--
miners, music, moonshine
cowboys, Mexicans, Apaches
lost mines, Terlingua...

No silver or gold unearthed in these vast lands,
yet alchemy lurked in the high desert plains--
The Troubadour listened,
gazed at the chameleon vistas,
and left the stone silhouettes for the eons.

Ode to the Washington Monument

Any fool can make something complicated.
It takes a genius to make it simple.
                              Woody Guthrie

Sleek, marble needle--
from above, "eyes" watch over
bureaucratic shrines.

Remembering Woody

A whirling dervish of shiny black vinyl--
a tiny needle alights on a slender landing strip,
finding its place in the spiraling grooves,
releasing a blend of chords, lyrics, vocals, harmonies.

This land is your land
This land is my land...

A populist anthem,
sung by the new folk singers
of the Fifties and Sixties,
each putting their mark
on the "Traditional Folk Song."

Christopher (Kit) Kelen's most recent volumes of
poetry are *God preserve me from those who want what's best
for me*, published in 2009 by Picaro Press, (N.S.W,
Australia) and
in conversation with the river, published in 2010 by VAC
(Chicago, USA). For the last ten years Kelen has taught
Literature and Creative Writing at the University of Macau in
south China.

---

hard working man and brave

Jesus is everything
heart and mind
wafer and wine
he is the very soul's biscuit
he is the sky affixed with pins
the needle eye man leading the camels
leaving the wives made salt
he is the unsmiling one
to whom the last laugh is yet
he is the hayrick harvest
of the barley moon
of the hickory rye
deep star draft night
and why?
not because sins are forgiven
not because fishes are bread
water wine
not even for a mother's grief
but because deep down
those bastard bankers preachers
will always be proud
they nailed him up

Cibyl Kavan is a housewife, mother and preschool teacher, both of which professions are economically marginalized occupations in our culture despite the twisted politically conservative rhetoric of "traditional family values"! She takes her sweet revenge by writing poems and songs about these "quotidian mysteries."

White Buffalo Woman Stirs the Pot

Her friends sit again
still as statues
absorbed in the invisible,
intoxicated on the moonshine

distilled from pain
and boredom.
Drunken thoughts blow
like tumbleweeds

across the open pasture.
Dandelion seeds scatter everywhere
motes of unwanted florid mind dust
uncompromisingly rooting

blooming, disfiguring
the pristine plane
of unclothed silence.
White Buffalo woman

stays home again. She stirs the pot
watching through the unbolted window.
An unobserved soup
of leeks and mushrooms simmers
on the back burner

the olive oil shimmering
in viscous, reflective puddles
across the top of the protean broth.

For dinner when
the sobered friends come to call
she serves a thick ragu
of word images. Of utterances, pictures

dreams, impossible laughter
stirred again and again
by the merest flick of her
white buffalo tail.

And then she cleans
The house. The toilets
And the bathtub, the dusty
Dining room. The towels folded. Neatly.

Daryl Ross Halencak was selected for an award by the Artist Embassy International Dancing Poetry Festival in San Francisco and the 2012 national competition sponsored by the Abilene Writers Guild. His non-fiction has been published in the Czech Republic and his poetry collection, *Staring Blue Eyes* was published in 2011. He lives in Crowell, Texas, where his family has resided for over one hundred years.

The Dirt Farmer

The dirt farmer bleeds sweat into
his planted fields.
The cotton withers within the red clay soil.
The dirt farmer
prays for a good crop-
enough of a yield to support his family.
But,
He knows that Wall Street and
City Boys control the price of his harvest.
He is a slave to the great, bowtie adorned masters
running the local co-op.
He is indentured to commodity boards
located far away from his piece of Heaven.
In spite of the grave obstacles,
in spite of the physical torture, the grueling labor,
he remains a believer in the American dream
because
he served his country well
when the draft board came knocking on his door.
He pays his taxes to the best of his abilities.
He pledges allegiance to the flag
under which he was born.
He is devoted to the grand concepts of equality regardless
of ethnic identity or religion or class.

Draped by such values, he desperately tries to understand
and to stand strong
and, yet
he utters unto himself when no one is listening-
"Is there really One Nation Under God with Liberty and
Justice for All?"
In the dead of his sleepless nights,
he questions his dogma.
In times of his economic woes
when he has trouble putting food on the table,
he cries out.
No one hears his feeble, shaky voice.
The dirt farmer searches for the promised economic
justice for all-the core belief in the true pursuit of happiness.
But,
how can one be happy with hungry bellies?
Unpaid bills?
Artificially low crop prices?
\He remains a devoted, card-carrying citizen,
Even though his heart of hearts reminds him that
his country has abandoned the family farmers.
He is told by the politicians that,
in the Land of the Free and the Home of the Brave,
capitalist principles will win and
the war against the family farmer
 will cease.
The end of the market-driven struggles will arrive
when the market corrects itself
All will be well with the world.
So they tell to the dirt farmer.

Dorothy Alexander is a poet, publisher, and storyteller. Born on the plains of western Oklahoma in the middle of the Dust Bowl and the Great Depression, descendant of Yellow Dog Democrats and card-carrying Socialists, she has been a social activist since the 1950s.

Come home, Woody Guthrie, Come home

Things are bad . . . again,
          and we need you.

Jesus is on the no-fly list, profiled as a terrorist.
It's the skin color and the hair, I guess.
Or, maybe, the sandals, the robes,
the piercing eyes, the wrong questions.

Plus, there are socialist accusations
I am afraid he's done it up brown this time.

We are afraid for the children, the old,
womankind, the poor, for queer folk,
outsiders of all stripes. The fracturing,
. . . like the war, . . . goes on . . . and on.

Money changers are bunking in the temple.
Lightning is flashing beyond the distant hills.
We can hear shouts and guttural threats,
rumors of morality mobs & pitchforks

So, Woody,
          if you can see your way clear,
we'd appreciate you bringing your machine
and giving us a hand here.

Sacrament

He came to us in the dusk
each day, my father,
sweat stained,
smelling of honest work,
dust on his face, his hair,
the cracked skin of his hands,
and always that burn of wind
around his eyes.
In her kitchen my mother offered
him cool water, while we waited
and watched him slake his thirst,
waited for him to acknowledge us,
his children, to say each of our names,
almost a benediction.
We brought another pail of water,
poured it into an enameled basin,
stood and watched him wash away
the grime of the fields.
When he finished,
we sat down at a rough table
and ate a plain meal
wrested from the dry soil
by his labor, his steadfast will.

Gay Agenda

Without it black people would still be picking cotton,
Hillary Clinton would be at home baking cookies.
Clarence Thomas would not be a Justice, not be married
to his own wife, nor could either of them cast a vote for
Brother Romney, who, by the way, would have NO civil
rights either, if not for that sinister Gay Agenda,
The Constitution of the United States of America!

Elaine Barton grew up on a small family wheat farm in western Oklahoma where they grew their own food and supported the family, an almost impossible accomplishment in this age. Her poetry appeared in *The Heart's Journey*, cancer journaling group, by Village Books Press, and *Travelin' Music, A Poetic Tribute to Woody Guthrie,* Village Books Press.

The "Ribbon of Highway" Ends

Whether it is the inevitability of the coasts or the fatigue of traveling the twists and turns of life, it ends. Suddenly like driving to the coastal highway where you can see all your beginnings and endings crash high against the rocks, or slowly, an in-land bay where high and low tide provides miles of perspective, preparedness, waiting on the breath in and out, bringing todays shells, debris, seaweed, never stepping in the same surf twice.

There are as many ways to go as roads to travel criss-crossing, cross-words, laments and those dread bucket lists, always about yesterday. If you are reading this and as far as you know you do not have Huntington's Disease, Lou Gehrig's, cancer, emphysema, multiple sclerosis, stroke, heart attack, or survived a debilitating injury, then that was yesterday but yesterday you didn't do anything, no nothing, to guarantee your longevity.

It's always good to have good genes. If you're rich and a control freak you can have your DNA code deciphered and some small degree of 'knowing' available to you. But living in the uncertainty carefully enumerated in the morbidity and mortality weekly report still includes you and what are you going to do when you know and science has nothing to offer you but study after double-blind placebo-controlled unreplicable study.

If there are a thousand ways to die, Woody died misunderstood and judged which only contributed to his suffering, pain and confusion. Science has given us some vaccines and some cures and some effective treatments for chronic conditions but the odds and idiosyncrasies of the multitudes of factors which influence our health elude statistical significance more often than not, a straw man standing between us and mortality.

Clean water and antibiotics has done more, but it is all the kindness and compassion shown along the way and in the most welcome days. Life threatening illness reveals our true selves to the temporary nature of all things. It can clarify our values and speak of or seek out our real affections perhaps for first time. Struggling and dying is the most important time to love and move into the assurances of what makes us all the same.

Dying is the best time to let go of Power Ball and Mega Millions if you haven't already. Hitch a ride on the train to nowhere, no need to pack a bag, cause where you're going you don't need nothing but your soul and the memories of all the love you made. It was never about whether you jumped from an airplane or saw the Eiffel Tower, or swam with dolphins. The "Ribbon of Highway" ends when you realize you wouldn't want to "turn back"

Gary L. Brower, editor of Malpais Review, is the author of three books of poetry: *The Book Of Knots; Planting Trees in Terra Incognita; and For The Wild Horses Of Placitas; also a cd, Gary Brower Reads*. He is a director of *the Duende Poetry Series of Placitas*. He has worked with migrant workers and members of his family were migrant workers.

Apple Tramps

for E. Ray & Dorothy Craig,
& their daughter Levene.

At orchard harvest time,
my aunt, uncle, and their daughter,
took their old Buick to Yakima,
to work as "apple tramps."

Ladders to trees, they filled baskets
with perfect planets of the arboreal galaxy,
which spread for light-years of acres
into the space of Eastern Washington.

When picking season was done,
car packed with apples for home,
they headed back to north Missouri
for winter hibernation.

As the arms of cold winds embraced their farmhouse,
tree limbs piled with snow,
the pot-bellied stove, knight in black armor,
exhaled heat into the living room.
With my uncle on fiddle, aunt the piano,
their little girl twirling to the music,
they accompanied an apple pie

as it sang in the oven,
which, just before bed,
was divided into farm-plot wedges
for harvest by mouth.

In midnight quiet,
the full moon shone through the window,
projected tree-branch shadows
like shaky fingers
toward a basket of glistened apples
on the kitchen table.

The wind, out of breath after the snow,
let the moon hang between leafless trees
like a cat's eye marble
that turned shiny as Yellow Delicious skin,
while the family slept-
dreaming the roundness
of the world.

Joy Ride

(Rogue River Valley, Oregon, 1977)

The orchard owner's son,
teenage friend riding shot-gun,
drank beer, laughed,
joy-riding in his father' s Jeep,
down back-roads
of his father's lands.

The Undocumented,
real but illegal workers
with invisible lives in hidden migrant camps,
worked the huge pear orchards

along both sides of the dirt road,
occasional wives alongside husbands
in the high picking season, --
were startled as the Jeep careened
toward them in the late summer heat.

Workers stopped picking,
watched the speeding car,
took a drink of juice they had been sold
at high prices by the crew boss
who prohibited them
from bringing their own food and drink
into the hot fields.

As the teenagers approached
a large oak beside the road,
they decided- just for fun-
to run over a worker's lunch,
a white bundle in a basket
in the shade of the tree.

In an instant, the Jeep swerved,
its large-tread tires
crushing the bundle,
laughing teenagers
escaping down the road
in a swirl of dust.

In the rearview mirror,
workers ran, shouted.
A man and woman stood in tears
over their dead child.

When police arrive
at the *patron's* house
to investigate the death

of an American-born infant
of undocumented workers
doing back-breaking work for cheap wages
(where high profits from illegal labor
are perfectly legal),
it's like a family reunion,
back-slaps and coffee,
since the cops know
the rich orchard owner,
a pillar of the community.

Nothing will happen to the teens,
everything will happen to the weeping parents
who will be turned in to the *Migra*
to be whisked away to the other side of the border
from their dead son,
so they won't cause trouble,
so these illegals won't try something legal,
a chance only Death could give them
that will never be allowed.

The workers,
from what's left of their paychecks
after deductions for Social Security
they do not have,
for insurance they cannot get,
for taxes deducted but not paid
by their employer,
and to the *coyote* who brought them
to the orchards of Southern Oregon,
take up a collection to bury the child,
victims of survival
paying the journey
for a victim who didn't.

George Wallace is a poet and journalist from New York who has performed his work across America and in Europe. He has authored more than nineteen poetry collections. He teaches literature at Pace University and edits Poetrybay, an online poetry magazine, and edits Poetryblog, Long Island Quarterly and Walt's Corner.

'Turnabout Is Fair Play' Thanksgiving Rag

i don't have any desire to see rich people or criminals or
those who have manipulated the fate of millions for their
own benefit through the technicalities of a political system
they have bought lock stock & barrel pepper sprayed or
burnt like heretics at america's stake -- but there's always
a nice cold river in november we might dump them into
when a landfill a construction site a national park with
rattlesnakes or hungry bears just won't do the trick --
i mean once in a while it'd be nice to strike a blow for
fair play & turn the profit motive on its tail -- toss the
lawyers & bankers the corporate snakes stockholders
lobbyists & agents of corporate doom into the drink -- like
crates of british tea into boston harbor i mean not the san
gennaro festival dunk tank -- i'm just saying pitch 'em in
the harbor & watch 'em float around awhile -- remind them
the people don't take it all the time -- when you think you've
got things buttoned down the people rise up outside the gates
wearing indian suits & war paint -- whooping like all hell ready
to do some damage in a manner appropriate to the
circumstances –
how long they have took it & with such grace & patience!
o who could blame them! one thanksgiving morning all the
wise guys in their wall street suits bobbing like barrels of oil --
with their golden parachutes turned inside out – face down
in a mess of turkey bones empty wine bottles & meekly
floating condoms

Snow White Went Down To The 99% Store

snow white went down to the 99% store to buy her
kid some beans but beans cost two & sleeping beauty
only had one o what shall I do sd sleeping beauty &
newt (one of the seven dwarves) replied get a job quit
yr whining & furthermore go take a bath but there were
no jobs to be had the one eyed giant of the one percent
had shipped them all far far away where there were no
taxes & people worked for pennies on the pound (like
pigs in a barnyard) o snow white what shall you do well
she got a gig at big bad wolf's strip club & sex emporium
down by the river where newt & the boys pay $100 a pop
to touch her tits & now her kid's got all the beans he can
possibly ever eat & an appearance date in juvenile court

Geraldine Green has read and been published in the UK, USA and Italy. Her collections *The Skin* and *Passio* were published by Flarestack, *Poems of a Molecatcher's Daughter*, *by* Palores Publications. *The Other Side of the Bridge*, by Indigo Dreams, will be out 2012. She's working on her next collection, *Salt Road*.

She worked because

she lost her husband in '93
she lost her husband in '93
she worked sweeping floors
she worked grinding her hips
in front of beer-drinking men
so her son could go to college
so her daughter could have pretty shoes

she worked washing dishes at greasy sinks --
at bars & diners & high school cafeterias
watched shiny faced girls
on prom night swing
past with their
crop-haired boys

shy, or balls tight across
the dance floor hipping it with
the girls the girls the giggling girls
air hot with sex

she watched them from the kitchen door
while the boys ferried pretty
girls round the dance floor

like a destroyer with a yacht attached to it
she liked that thought

she always wanted to be a poet
she thought about poetry
went back to the pots and pans the smell of grease

she never earned enough

that phrase became a mantra to her

she worked so fucking hard!
she never earned enough.

Hal C Clark is a native Texan and a graduate of Texas A&M University. He spends his time reading, writing and travelling. He has been published in *Illya's Honey, Red River Review,* and several anthologies."

Our America

Who built this land,
forged the steel,
cut the timber,
raised the cattle, grew the crops?
(They weren't sitting in a big office.)

Who poured the concrete
to form the dams and the roadways?
Who made the parts
and built the cars?
(They weren't billionaires on Wall Street.)

Who taught the children,
cared for the sick,
fought the fires,
defended us from enemies and kept us safe?
(They didn't get a bonus for their work.)

Who cleaned the floors and hallways,
made the beds,
mowed the lawns,
drove the trucks and ran the trains?
(Many struggled to provide for their children.)

Who built this land?
Who came seeking freedom from tyranny?

Who seeks equality for all?
Can we find it, working together?
(The Constitution says we can.)

September 15, 1963

Who were they?
Four young girls
dressing in choir robes inside a church.

What was their crime?
The wrong DNA,
too much pigment in their skin.

What did they want?
to sing about their faith,
to share with their families,
to feel proud of who they were.

Their sentence:
Death by dynamite.

Executed this date by shrouded men.
No appeal.

J. C. Mahan, aka *Johnie Catfish*, an Edmond Okie poet, owns the Funky Hair Ranch Salon and enjoys pottery, painting, photography, and poetry. He hosts art shows, wine tastings, house concerts, and fund raising cook outs. Invites Facebook friends. If it isn't fun, don't do it.

Right About Now

Right about now, Momma's washing dishes
Staring out that little kitchen window
Into the black of the night and wondering.
'Cause she knows her boy's out there, somewhere.

He's out there hungry, looking for a job.
Out there desperate for a break or an easy place to rob.
He's trying to score some crack for his pipe.
Or he's serving time, making a bad turn come out right.

Maybe he's become a father too young
After never having had one of his own.
Or sick with an aching fever burning his head
Contracted aids and needs be confined to bed.

Could be suited up, armor-mounted, cruising Iraq
Or Afghanistan, with three months still to go
While PTS's growing in the back of his mind.
Be remembering the horrors of this for a long, long time.

And right about now, somebody's going to say,
Things are going to be getting better, any day.
Times are a changing for sure, justice will win out.
Everything's going to be all right, right about now.

Dad's sits, rocking by an old empty bed
Reminiscing, his little girl, all smiles and curls,
Wondering where can she be tonight? Where's she gone to?
What ever'll become of her? What are we going to do?

'Cause she's probably out all night running the streets.
Panhandling, hustling, and whoring just to make ends meet.
Bad boyfriends leaving her with burses and crying babies.
Everyday filled with fear, regret and a whole lot of maybes.

She could be a single parent working to feed her kids,
It's no fun, always hoping for some help and getting none.
Or trying to find a way that's not too hard or too dirty
Playing ball with the boss offering a raise, and him getting
flirty.

Maybe working her ass off in night school for a degree
Or doing a man's job better than all those men at work,
Gaining resentment and no respect with only half the pay
Making her wish she'd never been born a girl.

And right about now, some politician's going to say,
"Fellow Americans, I believe it's getting better every day.
Times are changing, civil rights are guaranteed and here to
        stay.
Vote for me and everything will be all right, right about now."

Well, don't give us your tired, poor huddled masses yearning
        to be free,
Nor send us your homeless and tempest tossed no more.
The lamp is dark and we're closing that big golden door,
'Cause we got plenty of our own homeless we can't seem to
employ.

And right about now, my welcome become worn out
Always happens when I stop talking nice and go to preaching

Letting me know it's time for moving on.
But before I go, let's sing some of them old songs.

"This land is your Land" or "A Change is Going to Come"
All hold hands and sway just like we're about to pray.
Then you can feel better about things and I be on my way.
But let me have just this one last thing to say.

Right about now is a good time to get involved
In making this land a better place for us all.
With the Hammer of Justice you could strike a blow
And ring the Bell of Freedom so everybody could know.

Let's double the teachers' pay, give kids the schooling they
     need.
Get rid of the politicians and the money brokers steeped in
     greed.
Invest in the common man and the higher common purpose,
Make the rebuilding our nation our combined focus.

James Coburn, is Oklahoma-born and a longtime journalist for The Edmond Sun. A resident of Guthrie, Coburn has written poetry for many years but has only recently been sharing his works with poetry groups. He lives with his dog, Tilly, and his cat, Carl.

Oklahoma Lynching

Mosquitoes tasted blood of white men
Standing shoulder-to-shoulder across the Cimarron River bridge.
Separation of color in black and white, west of Okemah.
A postcard reveals the 1911 mob lynching;
Laura Nelson and son Lawrence, 15, hanged from bridge.
Dead wooden planks, dry under footsteps.
I bet a few of the 50 spectators photographed the next day
Dragged mother, infant and son from court house jail;
Distant faces exposed to curious stare.
Sunday communion trickled blood of Christ touching lips.
Mosquitoes swarmed down river. Infant missing.
Communion quenched killers' Sunday best.
Murder played God.
White hands gripped rope tight to Laura's neck after gang rape.
Lawrence shoved from bridge.
Slam of gravity forces pants to dangle under naked feet.
Mosquitoes swarm down river,
Skim the edge, fester torch light of malice.
Muted faces of men, women and children
Stand gripping iron laced bridge a century ago.
You lynchers dead now with your waters of injustice,
I spit in your waters. I drink of justice for mother and son.
They said Lawrence shot Sheriff Loney in the leg.
They said a posse went with Loney to investigate a cow theft.

They said Lawrence saw the sheriff draw a gun.
His father pleaded guilty to the theft, taken to prison.
Laura tried to save Lawrence, saying she shot the sheriff.
False trigger of hope.
Postcards sold like slavery. Image set free.
Mosquitoes swarm down the river,
Skim the edge, fester torch light of malice.

Jane Holwerda's writings have been published in GSU, PMS, Poetry Motel, Out of Line, Sou'wester, River King, Hurricane Review, South Loop, The MacGuffin, Guilty Pleasures and Loosely Identified. With a doctorate in American Studies from Saint Louis University, she teaches for Dodge City Community College in southwestern Kansas.

Sunday, A.M.

They cut a straight line
as they walk, starched
stiff, toward a lord of life wafer
hands cupped from unmet
expectations and poorly counseled
demands of ladies' clubs,
coffee hours in basements, pinochle,
too much jello and not enough bread,
bible studies of Moses conducted by the Rev.
Johanson who skips Moses' infant ride
down the Nile, the redemption by the queen,
jumps right into Moses as tribal chief,
leading God's people:
Moses at the Red Sea, its parting;
the way
tired men led mules, women cradled babies, children
herded goats, as, with a single wave of his hand,
the burning pillar of God beside him, the Sea parted
for these to walk through and from the enemy army
closing in. The Rev.
Johanson never lingered too long on the next part—
forty years of desert walking, no map. Moses lost,
looking for that land of milk and honey; Miriam,
the sister, who probably tended the manna jars,
dead, no more to lead with tambourine, measure or song.

The Rev. Johanson never talked
about those folks
crossing and recrossing
the desert in silence. The good man
always led direct
from the Red Sea to the Galilee,
from somebody's war to next week's
blood drives, our food box
for the marginalized. Amen.
Amen, the church women
sigh, *amen*.

Jeanetta Calhoun Mish is a poet and writer; her most recent collection of poetry is the award-winning *Work Is Love Made Visible* (West End Press, 2009). She is the Editor of Mongrel Empire Press and a member of the faculty of the Red Earth Creative Writing MFA at Oklahoma City University.

1977, Seminole County

me and my best friend k.t. hurtled down
chug holed roads in her green Gran Torino,
racing almost as fast as our doped up hearts
our hysterical laughter counterpointed by the crash
of glass on rural mailboxes, my aim truer
after killing a bottle of Night Train Express
guzzled over ice in a Sonic cup
we wanted our lives
to go fast but every Sunday morning
strung-out and sore-jawed, we confessed
that all the crank in the world could
not give us the escape velocity we needed
while making plans to try again
on Thursday, just the same.

barefoot philosophy

out here with the warm dark earth
squishing up between my toes
I'm fearless. not even the lime green
horned tomato worm scares me despite
the way it rears up like a wounded dragon.
yet there are dangers everywhere: the yoyo
blade too close to my foot and like
the reaper's scythe it momentarily
becomes a metaphor instead of a tool.
a pygmy rattler lives under the squash
blossoms and when I walk by carrying
a bag of of bone meal, she hisses as if
the ashes of the dead were calling out.
even the fruits of the garden are risky—
the sanguine tomatoes are perilous nightshades,
peach pits have poisonous hearts, and the poke
sallet that has sprung up between the lilac bush
and the rose of sharon whispers constantly that
he is most delicious when blanched only once. he's
such a liar, but I know his ways. I am at home
in the garden, and the perils here are comforting,
real. understandable. ancient. reciprocal.
I know my place and my part. what I'd give
to make of the world a garden, again.

Jennifer Kidney is a free-lance scholar and the author of six poetry books. She conducts writing workshops for libraries and schools, and is an adjunct assistant professor for the University of Oklahoma. Secretary of her local Audubon Society, she writes a newsletter, "Bird Notes." She wins awards for poetry, technical writing, and brownie baking. She lives in Norman with three cats and her dog Lizzie.

Driving To California – 1974

The cowboy boots in the Amarillo sign
are aptly yellow. "Fastest Route
to the Coast" the sign proclaims.
Each time I drive to the city,
I long to follow Route 66
to the sea. In Arizona I'd stop
at every trading post getting
cheated for treasures: bracelets of tin
and turquoise, blue as the sky
or the thin places on the thighs of my jeans.
I'd gawk at giant rattlers in cages
at roadside snake farms and look forward
to rock museums, dream movies
and open my eyes on their scenes
all around me: saguaro cactus
and mountains in the distance. In the purple desert
west of Flagstaff, Indian ponies
would munch the sparse grasses
and pose for my photographs. At last
where the wintry Pacific boils
along the beach, a hundred times
my heart would fall from the brink
of the cliff: the sun sets there.
Through orange and olive groves,

promised land of milk and honey,
I'd pursue the undulation of the road
to San Francisco where narrow pink
buildings, exuberant, insane, cling
to a precarious existence on the edge of things.
I'd take the "loneliest road" back home,
bringing along turquoise, beach stones,
sequoia nubs, a sack of dirty clothes.
There would still be snow
from Wolf Creek Pass
on the underside of the car.
It would melt and become absorbed
in the gray cement of the garage floor.

Armed And Dangerous

Why does the National Rifle Association
keep calling me from the familiar area code
where I grew up? Do they believe
that because I now live in a red state
in more ways than one that I'll fight
for my right to carry concealed?
I don't have a gun and don't want one.
I'm not a hunter. I like to see my deer
in the woods, my ducks on the pond.
I've no desire to shoot them, even
for dinner, and I deplore the greedy predator
who discarded the corpses of wood ducks
and green-winged teal by the side of the road
to the river. What was the point of that?
To prove he's a good shot? If I had a pistol
and knew how to use it, my rapist
would not have disappeared into the dark.
He'd be identified and dead. My bullying boss
would be out of a job, and I'd gladly pick off
my neighbor who troops out to his stoop
shirtless, clad only in boxer shorts, to hawk
and spit in the grass. I look cute in my bathing suit
but our yards are not the beach
and there's only chain link between us.
If I were armed, I'd surely be dangerous
and my hit list would soon be endless.

Jessica Isaacs is Division Chair of Language Arts and Humanities at Seminole State College. She teaches creative writing, literature, and composition, and is the Director of SSC's Annual Howlers and Yawpers Creativity Symposium. She presented her poetry at the Southwest Texas Popular and American Culture Conference, Scissortail Creative Writing Festival, and 2011 Woody Guthrie Festival. She enjoys experimenting with form in writing, often combining cross-genre techniques of playwriting, poetry, and fiction.

Sharing Fries with Mary Jo

I got the call one Autumn afternoon,
    "I have a book about my brother,"
said the lady on the other end of the line,
    "and I'd like to know if it's any good."

Sure, I said. I'd be happy to have a look
and offer my advice. After all,
I was a creative writing professor.
I should know a little something
about good writing.

So, she came to sit with me the next afternoon,
and we shared an order of curly fries in my office.

    "I've kept a scrapbook for years," she explained,
as she opened a giant three-ring binder across my desk.
    "These are memories of my brother, Woody."

Page by page we turned through his life.
These were bits and pieces of memories
from a little sister of her older brother.
These were special moments, still intact

despite the social pressures and back-turnings of the years.
These were Mary Jo's reckonings of Woody's life.
These, too, were her reckonings
of his influence on her life.

Who was I to make any kind of judgment?
Who was I to be privy to these memories?
So all I said was,
            "He sure was lucky, that Woody,
            to have a sister like you,"
and shared my fries and catsup with the legend's biggest fan,
completely humbled and honored
to be part of the moment at all.

Carry Me

Carry me home when I fall.
Cover me with your promises
in the cold January nights;
rock me to sleep
when the March winds drive me crazy;
tell me you love me;
carry me home.

Hold my hand when my child screams;
hold my head when my parents die.
Carry me, Love,
when my knees
won't hold me up anymore.
Carry me home.

When the hard freeze comes,
and the ice takes over at last,
carry me, Love;
bring the quilts to our bed,
kiss my forehead, tell me you love me,
tell me good night,
lay me gently in the ground,
and carve your name in my headboard.

Bring me flowers in the springtime;
remember my favorites;
lay the red Indian paintbrushes at my head.
Tell me again all the reasons why you love me;
remind me that you're coming home,
soon, dear, so very soon,
and I will rest beside you,
once again.

Jim Spurr is the officially-appointed Poet Laureate of Shawnee, Oklahoma, where he lives with his wife, Aline. Jim's chapbook, *Open Mic Thursday Night,* was a finalist for the 2007 Oklahoma Book Award, and his latest book*, Hail Mary, On Two*, was a finalist in 2012. Jim has read with the Woody Guthrie Poets since 2005 when the group formed, and is a co-founder of the Benedict Street Poetry Readings in Shawnee, Oklahoma.

The Hound of Bakersfield:1934

" Join the union
  and quit takin' this shit. "

At all night gospel sings
in California valleys
dogs sit up in pickup beds.
Takin' in the sound.

Someone   heard one
singin' loud in the night
like an alarm above
the sound of early morning music.

It said, "I am the worker
that cannot lie.
I worked all week
to see the Eagle Fly.

It came on Friday.
After the long hours
and short pay.
Be me and howl at the dawn!"

The New Life

It was final. Just like that.
The world was upright and normal again.
Adults would go back to their old lives.
Those who had survived. But not us.
Children did not have an old life.
There would never be another war.
That much even we knew.
The 40's war had been too brutal, too huge, too cruel.
So. Could we find a life in this new, quiet world
that would be handed us? Rebuilt and intact.
Probably. Much had happened in the past
decade and much was waiting in the next one.
Some of us would ride the open road with Kerouac.
We would be as bewildered by the beats
as if they had rewritten the Bible,
the Declaration of Independence
and The Star Spangled Banner. All in one day.
We would be awakened by the living new
wild sound of Charlie Parker
and all the cool modern jazz and Be Bop we could find.
Rock and R&B were just around the corner
screaming at us too for once in our lives
"Misbehave before it's too late'.
Hear Jerry Lee Lewis take the ' bull by the horn'.
Watch Elvis catapult out of Memphis.
Read J. D. Salinger tell us to question all authority
from Radio City Music Hall to the Heavenly Gates.
From the back roads we learned
Woody Guthrie had been singing for 20 years
coast to coast that this land was our responsibility
....because we owned it. That was his message
to the world.

And it was from all this and more that we smiled
a long sort of an evil looking grin of self-confidence.
We would reject the preachy and the staid.
Some of the boundaries we would even redraw.
We were given a new world to embrace and occupy..
...to embrace and occupy.
...........To try not to damage .   At least try.

Jody Karr is a writer, artist, photographer and poet with a bachelor's degree in art and a master's degree in writing. She has received national and international awards in art and national and regional awards in writing and/or poetry. She has served as judge for art, photography, and writing competitions.

Nesting

Street people
like birds building nests
of newspapers and rags
in alleys.

Souls meandering in time
nesting mostly in silence
or in feathery voices
strange and faltering.

Rain fizzing down
on grey, staring faces
that search for crumbs
with watchful eyes.

Like so many birds
flocked together
perched on park benches
in papery wrappers.

Soup Line

Rain trickles down
on strangers
with hollow eyes
of shame

Soup line bound
and tainted
with untold tales
and blame.

They stand
in solemn silence
while people
stop and stare

In shoes that
nobody wanted
a coat no one
would wear.

Vacant eyes in
friendless cities
in nature's
ragged embrace

Soup line bound
and hungry
lost in the
human race.

John Graves Morris, Professor of English at Cameron University, is the author of *Learning to Love the Music* (Rose Rock Press, 1999), a limited edition chapbook, and *Noise and Stories* (Plain View Press, 2008), a full-length collection. His poems have appeared or will be forthcoming in *Jelly Bucket*, *Concho River Review*, *Acreage Journal*, *Cybersoleil*, and in *Ain't Nobody That Can Sing Like Me*, an anthology of Oklahoma writing, published in 2010.

Just Walking Dully Along:
*A Talking Blues During the Centenary
Of Woody Guthrie's Birth*

I watched a man drift down the street
like a balloon too air-dwindled
to whoosh though clearly released
from something, most likely his job.
In this hard-knuckle, minimum-wage town,
we expect hard times and tough breaks
as much as we like crackback blocks
and touchdowns to pile up every fall,
but something about him stirred me,
and I found myself in step behind him
while he gulped water from a bottle
as if he could never get enough,
weaving toward a retail Dumpster
that was pregnant with merchandise
recently removed from the discount bin.
From five feet away, he aimed the empty
at the trash can and missed badly,
the spent plastic plunking end over end
on the patched, chuckholed asphalt.
An impatient waiting driver roared
past him onto the street and sped toward
some important appointment, new tires

flattening the skittering container.
His shoulders bowed under the weight
of some burden, an ox too jaded to move
a final load too large to begin on.
He seemed lost, and even though
I was trailing behind him, I began
to superimpose onto him the one picture
I have ever seen of my grandfather,
a man bent over and blurry with age,
fancying, too, my own expression
one day blossoming into this man's.
Grandpa was a skilled carpenter
who had helped erect the railroad
north of here over 100 years ago,
and he was later fired from that job
in the gut of the last Great Depression,
the jovial strut that made a cousin
call him King of the Poop Deck gone.
He was too old to labor with hands,
too untutored to be able to learn
another trade to barter time for money.
My grandmother divorced him, and even
though he remained afloat ten years
more before death, he was decommissioned,
all that was stale and threadbare burred
into him like barnacles no one could scrape.

Having pictured my grandfather more
than this distressed man for many minutes
after Photoshopping the memory onto him,
I began to muse, red-faced, about
having possibly stumbled over a mistake
the way a TV detective might trip
over a corpse in some dark office,
that this man might have shattered
for another, and temporary, reason,

and I started peering at my watch,
wondering if I needed to be somewhere.
"Even if he were Grandfather's ghost,"
I pled with myself, "what can I do?"
As I turned and made my way back to my car,
work crews up ahead were demolishing
a slack building—old, faded, lackluster—
that had slumped away from the street
almost as if ashamed of itself.
Men ripped away drywall and pulled beams
down, jackhammering cement and reducing
the land to rubble that could be cleared,
reclaimed, and repurposed for profit.

John Vincent Rouleau, raised in a drafty Civil-War era home on the banks of the Saint Croix River, developed a great passion for the natural world. He lives in the San Francisco Bay Area with wife and daughter. He is an avid painter.

Remind Me

dear sister
in your alcoholic stupor
you drift into the fetid past
we shared as children

when i call
please
don't bring me back

there

remind me of the river
the change of seasons
the great migrations above us
we watched when so small
and innocent
and pure

remind me of crabapple trees
and plum
running from yard-to-yard
from dawn till dusk
with the neighbor kids

a long string of family dogs
and again

the river.

Juan Manuel Perez is the author of Another Menudo Sunday (2007), *O' Dark Heaven: A Response To Suzette Haden Elgin's Definition Of Horror* (2009), *WUI: Written Under The Influence Of Trinidad Sanchez, Jr.* (2011), and six poetry chapbooks. He is the 2011-2012 Poet Laureate for the San Antonio Poets Association.

It's Not Easy Being Greasy

"It's not easy being greasy,"
I could hear my father say
But did they call you "Mexican Grease"
Because of what you ate that day

"It's not easy being greasy,"
I could hear my father say
But did they call you "Mexican Grease"
Because of what is on your hair today

"It's not easy being greasy,"
I could hear my father say
But did they call you "Mexican Grease"
Because you work on cars all day

"It's not easy being greasy,"
I could hear my father say
But did they call you "Mexican Grease"
Because in onion fields you sweat and pray

"It's not easy being greasy,"
I could hear my father say
But did they call you "Mexican Grease"
Because bigots had no others words to say

What If It Happened In America?

Arizona's SB 1040

Whatever happened to
Truth, justice, and the American way
Whatever happened to
America, land of the free, the proud
Whatever happened to
Good neighbors, apple pie, and comic books
Whatever happened to
America, the great, grand melting pot
Whatever happened to
America, the beautiful, land of immigrants
A year or two down the road
From this dehumanizing law
The last of the immigrants in heavy, kryptonite chains
Arrested, deported, demoralized
The greatest of ourselves
Kal-El, the last son of Krypton

Immigration Reform #001

Is making sure that
American-made tacos
Represent their original ancestry
Rich, full of spice and flavor

Julia McConnell lives in Oklahoma City with her partner. She has a Masters in Library Science (University of Oklahoma 2011) She works as a public librarian, wears purple tights and cowboy boots to work, and devotes her free time to poetry.

These boots kill fascists.

My red cowboy boots are faded
like the cracked vinyl bench seat
in an old Ford truck.
Jackson Pollock splatters on one toe
from breaking up a dog fight.
Blood was flying everywhere
and I got more bites than the dogs.
A smear of tar on the other toe
from the parking lot
where we saw *Beauty and the Beast*
in 3-D and I took a hit in someone's car
just to feel a little less recycled.

The heels need fixing.
I've worn down the sole walking
heel to toe, clomping along, hips swinging
doing some kind of John Wayne swagger
like I think I am Woody Guthrie's spiritual
descendent, not a girl from the suburbs
who hasn't ridden a horse
in damn near twenty years and even then
it was on a girl scout outing.
We wore bicycle helmets while the horses
walked nose to butt down a well-worn trail.

I put on these boots like Clark Kent
becoming Annie Oakley.
Every morning I open the library doors

to job seekers who are waiting
to use the public computers.
I help them send their resumes
as email attachments
and to download
applications for assistance.
I go to work and find good clean books
for church ladies while I slip the grandkids
dystopian fantasies.
I think how glad I am to have
good teeth and a nice pair of shoes
in a state that's a red solo cup
and a strip mall.
This is my proof of address.

Reference Desk

Fred Moon calls the library to find out when the juice box was
invented.

Larry Marks calls the library like he is summoning a secretary.
"Honey, I need the number for the Chairman of Dean McGee –
not the CEO – I don't want to talk to that bastard."

Larry Marks calls the library the next day and asks for the
number for St. Vincent De Paul's thrift store and Castle Cab.
He needs new shoes.

Wanda Richardson wants to know if gambling is a sin. "We
were talking about it in church. Some people said it was but I
don't think so. What does the bible say?

Mr. Private calls the library from a blocked number. "You
know Boris Karloff? He hosted this show in the 60's, *Thriller*.
Did he act in it too?"

Mrs. Sanderson wants the number to make a complaint about the construction in Midwest City. "I'm new to this area and last week I paid a cab driver three hundred dollars to drive me all over the city and give me a tour. I treated him to lunch, dinner, and a little snack."

Cathy Smoot wants us to order a movie from the eighties where a boy gets a job delivering pizzas and kisses all the girls. "Mom wouldn't let me watch it in high school. Oh, and *Green Acres*, Mom loves *Green Acres*."

Larry Smith wants to know if you can put a dining table in a salon and still call it a salon.

Marty calls the library for a book on growth hormones in pigs. He wants to breed Godzilla pigs.

Joan calls the library almost every day to hear a recitation of the recipes demonstrated on the Food Channel from noon to three thirty.

Mr. Miller wonders if an actress from *Dark Shadows* is still living. How did she die? He then hangs up.

Bernice Dukes wants the number for roadside clean up. There is a dead cat on the intersection of Reno and Santa Fe.

Burt Lowell calls the library to ask if light can pass through aluminum foil. "I try to cover my windows completely – but the light is still coming through."

They call the library but never step inside. These faceless people are calling for a voice.

Julie Chappell, Associate Professor of Medieval and Early Modern British Literature at Tarleton State University, Stephenville, Texas, is an editor, translator and academic researcher with three books published. She reads her poetry and prose in various venues and several pieces have appeared in anthologies. A collection of poetry and a memoir are in progress.

Blue Plate Special

If, as Oscar Wilde once wrote, "art never expresses anything but itself."
Dali's crucified Christ is screaming in rage.

It is a silver plate with a raised figure of Christ on the Cross the Cross is collapsing over the top of the body of Christ whose concave chest and raised pelvis are the embodiment of Suffering an object much like an Easter egg lies silently in the lower left corner the crucifix has been put on the plate with silver dowels like extra nails or ones that missed the first time the soldiers tried to secure the man onto his death device the cold grey of the silver moves undisturbed across the mind in a pause to comprehend it.

Christ on a plate.
The ultimate food for human consumption.

A Blue Plate Special, a quick fix for the hungry, the disenchanted, the desolate, the poor, the hopeless fresh today with a side of false piety and with dissembling humility for dessert to ingest and discharge again well-chewed and re-formed.

The Cross collapses under the weight of its blasphemy.

Rhubarb

Call us rhubarb, if you must,
and not woman;
we are not part of man
with our veins full red and sweet.

We are not spelled with a "y"
to change our connection
our color, our gender
to alter our sexuality.

We do not cry for a penis

we're missing nothing
in our carefully contrived space
in our discrete selves.

Marginal to existence
like the bittersweet rhubarb stalk
we nourish all and yet
digest us uncooked, unmutilated
and we'll stick in your craw.

We'll choke you in your greed
your indifference to our uniqueness
and in the agonizing death of your convulsions
you'll feel our sweet, full red at last.

Nota Bene

Old, white men writing our history
robbed us of our due
perpetuated themselves as deities
to be honored, praised, and gratified,
justifying their rape and pillage
of our Selves.

We, who were not old, white men,
too often bowed our heads in supplication
at the altar of our shame
built with our own degradation
and sanctified with our sweet blood.

Armed with the sword of
god-sent superiority and righteousness
old, white men blinded us with their symbols,
maimed us with their rhetoric
killed us with their pure, white hands.

Insignificant in our martyrdom
we, who were not old, white men
remained agoraphobic and
in the closet of our ignorance
cowered from our intellect

the one, true power of our divinity.

But domesday has come at last
and old, white men
with their deceptions and abuses hanging out
stand naked and exposed
the blood still dripping,
fresh on their white hands.

Kathamann, a retired Peace Corps Volunteer in Afghanistan and a registered nurse, has been involved in painting and sculpture in the Santa Fe arts community for thirty years and has been published in *Waving; Not Drowning, Sage Trail, The Rag, Lunarosity, Beatlick News, When Red Becomes an Apple, The House Where Numbers Slept, Small Canyons II, III, IV, and V Anthology, Chest, Echoes, Malpais, The Enigmatist, Adobe Walls II and III,* and many others.

The Many You's and I's.

Sowing the secrets of the sea.
Satisfied my battle is done.

30,000 flies in grassy grass grass
a folk song for buffalo gals

my car, car Cadillac eight hesitates.
Lonesome 90 mile wind.

Remember poor boys and red wine.
Hear the mermaids roll on little
            ocean.

In pastures of plenty waiting
            at the gate.
Sleep eyed Sally Goodin.

Rolling in the wheel of life.
Daddy doesn't know your name.

I take my penny and little seed
            to the lonesome valley.

Buffalo skinners love little saka sugar.
Rollin oil eases my revolutionary mind.

Dry bed in east Texas red.
I was born in the House of the Rising Sun.

Sinking of the meanest man.
An ocean of peaceful swims my swims.

Good to know Oklahoma Hills.
One by one the old folks pass away.

Holy ground in heaven knows my soul.
So long its been a pin boogie.

Kell Robertson was born to a poor farming family in Kansas. His alcoholic father abandoned him and his abusive alcoholic step-father forced him onto the street at thirteen. Kell became a wanderer and, inspired by the music of Hank Williams, he learned to sing and play guitar. After years of itinerant living he became a poet publishing chapbooks here and there. During the 1960s and 70s, he became part of the literary scene in San Francisco, performing with poets and musicians of the Beat scene such as old Wobbly poet Utah Phillips, Jack Micheline and others. Lawrence Ferlinghetti said of Kell's poetry: *I would say that Kell Robertson is one fine . . . poet, worth a dozen New Yorker poetasters. Let them listen and hear a voice of the Real America out there.* Kell published some twelve chapbooks of poetry. His best known work is: *A Horse Called Desperation* (San Francisco, Aspermont Press, 1995).

He produced three CDs of his own music he wrote, arranged, sang and played: *When You Come Down Off The Mountain; Cool And Dark Inside;* and *Cause I'm Crazy.* All his original work is out of print; however, thirty-eight pages of his best work appears in the poetry quarterly *Malpais Review* (Vol. 1, No. 4, Spring, 2011) where he was featured; and in MR, Vol. 2, No. 3 (Winter, 2011-12), a memorial segment after his death in November, 2011. *Malpais Review* is edited by Gary Brower, a contributor to this anthology, who knew Kell and who submitted Kell's poem, *For Woody Guthrie.* The poem appears here by permission of Argos MacCallum on behalf of Penny Read, Kell Robertson's daughter, and the Kell Robertson Estate.

Kell lived in New Mexico during the last twenty years of his life and he sometimes played and sang live on Saturday nights at a Santa Fe radio station. At the time of his death he lived in a little house built for him out of an old chicken coop, on rural land owned by friends south of Santa Fe, still typing out poems on an old manual typewriter.

For Woody Guthrie

Out of the dust
coughing
 toward the cool waters
 of California
your people
my people
 Charlie Arthur Floyd people
 your voice
 a dry spell on the plains
 a rusty nail
 a creaky windmill
 songs with hard words
 dry throats
 working man's hands
 right down on the ground
 walking on grandma's grave
 and a scorn for
 laws to make money from
 music
 that music
 which came out of
 the hard times of people

And the face of a starving child
turns into dollars
for slick eyed boys
stars only
when the rhinestones glitter
under the spotlights

But back there
Zapata swings his rifle around
you play your guitar

sing everybody's songs
and the eyes of man
retain the fire
to fix the fences
or burn the world down

Ken Hada is a Professor at East Central University where he directs the annual Scissortail Creative Writing Festival. He has three collections of poetry: *The Way of the Wind, Spare Parts* and *The River White: A Confluence of Brush & Quill,* a collaboration with his brother Duane's *plein air* watercolors, tracing the White River from its source in northwest Arkansas 700 miles downstream to the Mississippi River.

Great Grandpa Gustava

He was conscripted into the Kaiser's army once
before, so when they came knocking a second
time, he married Julia and got the hell out
of their Hungarian home, took a honeymoon

trip to Ellis Island, never to return. He was
a crack shot, but in Oklahoma he preferred
to walk pastures every day calling his cows
by name, recording their refugee lives

flourishing in buffalo grass and gyp water
flowing through Greenleaf Creek. His collar
was buttoned to the top, a pipe curling
from his chapped lips rested on his chest.

For Julia, he translated the newspaper to
Hungarian, but refused to speak to salesmen
or unwanted visitors: "No English. Talk boy"
he would say pointing to one of seven sons.

After so much nonsense, he would bark
his custom cryptic phrase: "Go to hell, shit!"
Thus ending the exchange, thus keeping
a capricious world from tipping out of balance.

Tire Swing

It hangs from a Cottonwood near Mud Creek.
I'm surprised this tiny outlet has a name
although now the muddy water
is bruised with oil sludge.

The tire swing hangs limp.
The frowning Cottonwood remembers
times when a young dad strung the rope
and tied a bald tire in place.

A fun-making dad, adored
by his child swinging on summer afternoons,
Oklahoma wind lifting
the tire, the boy squeaking in delight.

Both are gone now:
An old man hardly remembers anything
except debt, foreclosure
and a dream that never woke.

The boy sits in an office cubicle
in Duncan keeping Halliburton
relevant. His tours of duty
in Iraq, his weekend warrior-ship

are the closest things now
to childhood adventure – those first days
swinging strong, flying high
above Mud Creek – free and clear.

A Road

I lay down with thunder,
Pines whistle above me.
A tiredness takes over
        like waves upon the sand.

        I see the good of my
        life is not mine at all –

as Chuang Tzu observes:
*A road is made by people
walking on it* – and a poem,
like a life, is drafted
at the mercy of that
which is unseen.

Lana Henson is an actress and singer who lives in Oklahoma City. She has been writing poetry since she was a child. She does metal sculpture for a living so that makes her a starving artist all around. She has been to every Woody Fest.

Hot July afternoon

sun beating down on the fields
wind blowing through your hair
the strains of Woody Guthrie on the air

Blue clouds turn to gray
the wind picks up
thunderstorms on the way

The horizon golden behind the violet clouds
Ellis, singing "God's Promise," says
Bob is working the lights

The sky darkens and rain falls
moved by the spirit of music and the elements
we dance in the rain as Ellis' voice soars

We are lifted on the spirits of Woody and Bob
a magical Okemah night.

Oklahoma Reverie

July evening in Okemah
yellowed fields of cracked red earth
the heat shimmers visibly in the air
along with the strains of the Burns Sisters

As Ellis Paul take the stage,
the sun begins to set bringing some relief
in the west the sky is painted
gold, pink, purple, and blue
while in the east an almost full moon appears
as if on cue, Ellis sings in "Anna Lee"
of the full moon rising

Another Woody Fest has begun
where the faithful brave the dust and heat
to gather in song
and in the spirit of Woody Guthrie.

Larry D. Thomas, 2008 Texas Poet Laureate, whose
tenant-farmer grandparents came from Tennessee to West
Texas by covered wagon in the late 1880s. His parents picked
cotton until their mid-thirties when his father went to work
at a service station.

Hard Wine

Their shotgun shacks
are hidden in the shadows
of skyscrapers,
their roof shingles
black as the ink
of desolate headlines.

Life drinks them
like hard wine
as crows' feet
deepen near their eyes.
Days, they labor
for bags of beans and rice,

and till little gardens
sparkling with shards
of broken glass.
Nights, in minutes
of hard-earned bliss,
their bedsprings creak

with the rhythm
of fine Swiss clocks
ticking their lives away,
ticking miles away
on the elegant mahogany
mantels of their bosses.

The Ploughmen

Their daughters,
to save themselves from the black,
stampeding mares of the night,

clutch for dear life
their cabbagehead dolls.
For the sake of a good harvest,

they read Bibles
paged with the skin of onions,
blow out their lanterns

with the breath of fresh garlic,
and dangle carrots
from the rafters of their prayers.

In the heirloom
turnip watches of their fathers,
their hallowed lineage ticks.

American Gothic
(painting by Grant Wood)

Their faces
are dried,

wrinkled, plain
as The Plains

of their handiwork.
The gentleman

is fixed
with a pitchfork:

the lady,
clad to her adam's

apple:
an Iowa

couple
whose last juices

fester
in the wound

of a marriage
flawlessly sutured
with brutal,
catgut sorrow.

Loretta Diane Walker received a Bachelor of Music
Education degree from Texas Tech University and earned a
Master's of Elementary Education from the University of
Texas at the Permian Basin. She currently teaches music to
elementary children at Reagan Academic Magnet School in
Odessa, Texas.
Her work appears in various publications. Her book *Word
Ghetto* won the 2011 Bluelight Press Book Award.

Barriers

> *That makes me as happy as hash browns and brownies.*
> *--Jeremy Witherspoon*

His four year old smile is the flesh of innocence
while he dangles his legs like a ragdoll.
The view from his mother's hip is better,
the world safer, kinder, smaller near her heart.
To see the sky with arms wrapped around her neck
is happiness like hash browns and brownies.
Not like the taste of fear in my mouth
as I watch this politician running with spite on his heels.
His words are harpoons aimed at the vulnerable.

How he desires to wash away the poor.
Sweep them under the stoop of arrogance.
Spray them with a hose of insignificance.
Let them drain into the sewage of nonexistence.
And those in the middle—the ones with two slices of bread
and no butter, he will instruct them to collect toothpicks
to build new cities.
Prick them with the points until blood fills
the cracks of division.
For those with enough but cannot buy a country,

what fate will he assign them?
If we all disappear, return to that place before conception
where earth and water are not separate,
what will be wealth's measuring rod?

There is a green lady standing at the shore
with a flamed hand burning with hope,
broken shackles of oppression and cruelty at her feet.
Oh, how this soul desires to sit on her hip
and listen to the stories of dreams rolling in and out to sea.

Malcolm Willison has been writing, presenting, and
publishing poems for quite a while, particularly in the
Northeast, Key West, and New Orleans, along with teaching,
editing, and working on social justice and peace issues

The Crash

It started unraveling where you still felt
pretty good, despite an exuberant nose
for a killing getting raw, with a nice flush
to the system despite some handy
pronouncements and prescriptions—
you were toasty in bed with regulators
and not yet toast yourself
before the dominos
began their fall.

Your head had not yet begun to swell
with anticipation more than it already had
or the margin of your nose to hollow out
like a blown conch shell alert
though you began
to feel sub-prime.

You only hope the harried telephone calls,
the palliatives, etceteras, hurry to relieve
some symptoms, or that you can eventually hide
opening your eyes only once in a while
to someone taking your temperature
one end or the other, while looking
at your chart with not too much
concern or irony.

Presages

In brand-new paneled stateroom suites
those weighted with their wealth are
quarreling. Gamblers at cards
are busy with their chips. Cigars
in the smoking room glow with risqué stories.

Long past dinner at the captain's table
the grand saloon is slowly emptying
of casual conversation.
Plans for arrival at the great city early
are being made at purser's late-open office.

Deep within the long slender hull
so lately proudly launched
giant boilers roar at stokers' heave
to beat a rival line to gain
the plaudits of the portside press.

Each bulwark, ready to seal off the next
stands higher than any other ship's
for safety's sake and proud design.
Only lifeboats have been skimped
for wider outlooks on the promenade.

The Palm Gardens have seen
who of the refined are gracious
to their servants, and who cruel
toward those who trespass
on the Persian rugs.

On the sleek decks, late strollers
turn their sleeves down and collars up.

Bad luck at the departure from propellers'
powerful suction almost-accident
to other ships by now's forgot.

Onward through the night
like a dreadnought
the liner churns its wake,
slicing the dark
with its slim bow.

Lookouts man binoculars high up
in the crow's nest, and semi-heeded
messages crackle post-closing-time
of what's ahead, before most sleep
into the unwary's sudden cry.

Maria Polson Veres has published poetry in *Epiphany, Edgz, Main Street Rag,* and many other magazines. Her first chapbook, *Waiting for Miracles*, was published by Village Books Press in 2007. A previous Woodyfest reader, she is Vice President of Oklahoma Writers Federation. Visit her at mariapolsonveres.com.

Princess of the Doublewide

They give her everything
possible. A rusting swingset,
sandbox, third-hand trampoline,
a drawerful of hair-bows.
When the thrift store runs a sale—
fill a bag for only $5—
they choose the necessary T-shirts,
sweatpants, jeans
a jacket with a ripped sleeve
but in that $5 bag, they always make room
for a pair of high heels
gold or red or white satin.
She owns two overflowing boxes
of dress-up shoes, more
than all her friends.

Moving Forward?

Brown-skinned guy
trims a hedge in Richland Parke.
Lexus pulls up, window glides down.
"How—much—*money*
do you—*charge*
to *mow*—a *yard?*"
Brown-skinned guy says,
"I live here."
Lexus lady snaps the window closed.
Next day a For Sale sign graces her lawn.

Mark A. Fisher is a writer, poet and playwright. He is an Okie now living in Tehachapi, California, a small town nestled at the southern end of the Sierra Nevada Mountains between the "pastures of plenty" of California's Central Valley and the "diamond desert" of the Mojave.

drifter

on the road
I watch the fences
laid out, marking grids
– checkerboard lines
cast like nets
across empty fields
hauling a big
catch of freedom;
where tumble down towns
watch main street go dark
as boom times
fade away
remembered only by
old men –
talking
in empty cafes
and dreams have blown
the young away
to gather in the cities
like tumbleweeds –
in gridded streets
snared by an illusion
of freedom;
while I listen
to the meadowlark
– singing
beyond the fence

over the rainbow

desolate rainbows
cast across the empty
highways to LA;
where dreams come
to die.
people passing through
scenery
feeling lost,
thinking that they'll
find answers at
the end of the road.
their empty pots
drained of gold,
until they really are
lost.
surrounded by others
all looking with
twinkles
in their eyes,
for some way out,
without going
home.

Mark Evans, taught in public schools and night school at Oklahoma State University for 27 years. He served as a writer and editor for Economy Publishing Co. and as freelance writer for publishing companies. When a young man, he worked as a janitor and day laborer, and logged many miles hitchhiking across the country meeting people, rich people and poor, in both money and spirit. That gave him his real education.

Workhorse

diggin' through the work day trash
to find the cash to make it through the month
tryin' to avoid the bill collector crunch
too beat down to see
who or what is doin' this to me
can't hear me scream cause I got no voice
too beat up to even make a choice
too tired for work
too old for school
tryin' not to lose
what's already lost
got a home and car
But can't pay the cost
I'm not middle class
I'm a little bit lower
but my 1% master
can kiss my asterisk
cause I may be old and poor
but I'm a hell of a fighter
better watch out, boys,
I'm 99% workhorse
and I'm about to buck the rider.

pledge

I pledge allegiance to the corporations of America,
And to the franchise employment opportunities
And the guaranteed minimum wage
For which they stand
And to shopping malls and golden arches
And corporate business models
From sea to shining sea.
Wall Street has shed its grace on me.

And I pledge obedience to the USA
And to the IRS and the DEA and the FBI and the FTA,
And to homeland security, for whom I stand
And assume the position,
And to the other agencies
Designed to watch over me
And to protect me from certain mayhem
As long as I obey them.

And I pledge compliance with the laws of the United States
And with the leaders who make them
And with their corporate sponsors
And the loyal consumers who elected them,
May they all grow fatter,
One nation, under free market Capitalism,
With an acceptable standard of living
For all who matter.

Mary A. Grijalva-Bernal has writen poetry and short stories for over 60 years while supporting herself, first as a clerk, then a legal secretary, and finally a paralegal in Phoenix, Arizona before retiring to San Diego, California. She has six children, 16 grandchildren, and 12 great-grandchildren.

Now is the Time

Now is the time, and this is the hour,
America's courage is ready to flower.

Truth is our sword, God's love our strength,
We can walk every step, no matter the length.

It does not matter when or where we began,
As long as we all give as much as we can.

Men can have differences and still be brothers,
They can shape their destinies by helping others.

In our country we all have the biggest stake,
If multitudes help, what a difference we'll make.

From every walk of life, we must give our all,
We must protect the masses, answer the call.

What matters is that we love our neighbor,
And, always, be ready to do him a favor.

Our ability to reach out to another's need,
Who is in dire want of loving deed.

Our freedoms are worthy of the extra task;
Everyone's charity and love; that's all we ask.
 Many times before many have given their lives,
And, with each other's service, we did survive.

We owe it to those who gave us our liberty;
Let's prove that we are worthy of this dignity.

Just as our forefathers who gave their all,
We can do it again, stand straight and tall.

To all who believe, it's a fact well-known,
That we shall reap just what we have sown.

Michelle Hartman has been published in *Raleigh Review*, *San Pedro River Review*, *Pacific Review*, *Concho River Review*, *Main Street Rag Journal*, *Texas Poetry Calendar*, *Eclectica*, *Sojourn*, *Aries*, *descant*, *RiverSedge*, *Mirror Dance*, *Illya's Honey*, several anthologies, and was a juried poet in the 2009 Houston Poetry Festival. She is the editor for the online journal, *Red River Review*.

in the great god's hair

I am drinking coffee from my
disappearing civil liberties mug—
on which the Constitution disappears
when a hot beverage is added
same way I wish I could disappear
when propaganda is pored

I try to figure when Jesus
jumped the shark, got
into government work

and gutted the Bible raking
all the blessings to himself
ladled damnation to
the rest of us, his words goo
my ear, plop down to my shoulder
leave greasy stain on my shirt

is it too late for ninety-five post-it notes
on the door—
a cafeteria of carnage in the Middle East
to gain a nickel's worth
of God's attention

it will take an iamb of poets to redeem us
they are the black holes
we should be researching
words sucked into poems
blown into another universe
where someone—maybe
will hear our plea

Dirty business of fairy tales
after Malcolm Pryce

some bingo hall hustler thinking to make
his fortune traveling with the spinning
wheel Sleeping Beauty pricked
her finger on; didn't reckon on Oklahoma
farm girls and rich urinal cake heiresses trying
to spin the big wheel for fame and love scores
known as treadle trollops ending up trading soft
white skin to men more frog than prince
in exchange for food or a substance more
soothing in the dark recesses of night
spindle spinsters, waiting forever
or the government seizing damned machine
billions spent on R&D con men trying to spin gold
while leprechauns, dwarfs and ogres show up day
after day accompanied by slick solicitors
and hey-boy hawkers bearing ownership claims

and the hustler wearing the same smile sported
by under-taker, pimp and others with a professional
understanding of the hearts of men
closes a lucrative book deal
a story cleaned up by the movie industry
spoon-fed to another generation of girls

The political season

I wonder what Ayn
Rand would have thought of Bernie
Maddow's individuality?

god don't need no hell

        don't need no lucifer
to run it for him
got straw bosses on crews laying tar
in houston—in august
picking okra in the valley
peaches in georgia
wife working uptown
wiping shit offen the bottoms
of their young and old
he got welfare christmas
ain't nothin' hurts like
not takin' care of yer kids
and there's cancer
and emphysema and parkinson's
anything that rots yer guts
whilst yer family watches
and waits knowing they can't pay
the undertaker hovering
like death watch beetle
and the rich folks preachin'
family values, stopping
abortion cause hungry mouths
keep a man down
so they got heaven and we got hell
and we don't need no god neither

Mimi Moriarty is the poetry editor for *The Spotlight,* a weekly newspaper in the Albany, NY area. She has two chapbooks published by Finishing Line Press: *War Psalm;* and *Sibling Reverie,* co-authored with her brother, Frank Desiderio. A third chapbook, *Crows Calling,* will be published by Foothills Press.

A Man Your Age

You'd think a man your age would know
which direction the wind blows

you'd think a man with a fertile mind
would practice the art of caution

when to hush your hunk of tongue
when to pocket your ballpoint pen

a man your age would brace yourself
against a mutiny, honors given

honors taken away, so watch your words -
Boy - watch those words - war, greed, poverty

drop them from your lexicon, repeat after me -
Birdsong, Violets, Honey Bee

> *the root of your problem, the painted truth*
> *as you perceive it, the right to repeat it*

a man your age should not be shocked
to be stripped, from collar to shoelace,

of honors bestowed by a silent nation
for your small poems about the end of the world.

Chambers

In one I hold Viet Nam
in another Iraq
these chambers full

who would believe
the fiction we ask
our soldiers to write

we ask them
to swallow stones,
we ask them

to scrawl the names
of the dead
on monuments

they spend countless
birthdays alone
in Veterans'

hospitals with
aching, amputated
limbs, and when

they complain we urge
them to crawl into
yet another chamber

liquid amber ready
to harden around
them, years later

when their absence

is no longer felt
or noticed, we

will pick up the golden
husk of memory, admire
framed portraits

of soldiers who served
in Viet Nam and Iraq
place the artifact next

to our own fossilized
guilt on shelves, their
absence a mere

happenstance of history
forced into one last chamber
like a bullet.

Lever

Tomorrow I will vote for town officials
who will fix my roads and haul my trash

I will pull the lever over the name Grant
or Stanton, Hollinger or Schute.

My town, my board, my justice
of the peace, my choice.

Where is the lever over peace, not war?
Where is the lever over No More War?

Where is the lever over No More Iraq?

Where is the lever over Please, not Iran?

I stand in the park with my sign
you already know my sentiments

fixing my roads is important
hauling my trash is important

but my neighbor's son has been sworn in
and I want to pull the lever

my cousin's husband is MIA
and I want to pull the lever

the National Guard is in the desert
and I want to pull the lever

my grandson is playing with guns
and I want to pull the lever

before he is sworn in and sent
to the desert - he is only six

I want to pull the lever
because if we should be voting

for anything   it is this.

Nathan Brown is a singer-songwriter, photographer, and award-winning poet. His many published works include *Two Tables Over*, winner of the 2008 Oklahoma Book Award, and *Karma Crisis: New and Selected Poems,* his latest collection (2012). He is the author *of Letters to the One-Armed Poet, A Memoir of Friendship, Loss, and Butternut Squash Ravioli,* short nonfiction pieces celebrating the late Jim Chastain, a fellow poet.

Making Amends

...according to their respective Numbers, which shall be determined by adding to the whole Number of free Persons, including those bound to Service for a Term of Years, and excluding Indians not taxed, three fifths of all other Persons.
— *The Constitution of the United States of America, Article. I. Section. 2.*

I'm surprised
the Founding Fathers
couldn't have seen them coming,
all those Amendments to the Constitution,

that those Persons they considered fractions
wouldn't want, someday, down the road,
to be counted as Whole,

or that the Excluded might want to keep
the land we were prying them from,

and that Women, so uncounted
as to even escape mention,

might not desire the Privilege
to vote their Founding Asses
straight out of office.

Norma Wilson, Professor Emeritus of English, University of South Dakota, is author of *Wild Iris* (poems) and *The Nature of Native American Poetry* and co-editor of *One-Room Country School: South Dakota Stories*. She holds a Ph.D. in English from O.U. and values her ties with the red bud state.

Renewing Our Energy

Dinosaurs bob their heads up and down
sucking all they can get of the red earth's
blood so some tycoon, born yet again,
can drive his Hum Vee in liberty.
Who cares that carbon dioxide goes up
and trees are downed?
Not he with the mantra, "Drill, baby drill!

Filthy with lucre, the giant thinks he deserves
what he wants to control—the bodies
of Earth and all her children.
He rips out the trees and mines the sands
for dirty crude. He devised a stint
to pipe that tar down through the plains,
but friends of the Earth said "No!"
Circled our White House, and sang
for the land and waters across this land.

Now the giant has another plan.
He'll pipe that crude from Oklahoma
to the Gulf of Mexico to be shipped
on tankers to China. The money
rolls in tax free, while we pay more
for his drilling spree.

Friends of Earth say, "No more CO2
or carcinogens. No more blood for oil!"
Let ballet dancers on wind cartwheel
above the plains renewing our energy.
May the wind and sun heal our Earth.

Respect the Key

"I have heard of many *English* lost, and have oft been
lost my selfe, and my selfe and others have often been
found, and succoured by the *Indians*.
   --Roger Williams, *A Key into the Language of America.*

Twenty years ago the first Mexicans
were welcomed by the First Baptists.
But the Mexicans wanted to pray and sing
in their native tongue. They built
the Cristo Rey Spanish Baptist Church,
a white steel building with red neon cross
on the other side of town.

Soon there was a Mexican restaurant
on Main Street, and the Mexican
immigrants' children began to excel
in school, graduate, and enter college.
The oil field workers saved money
and bought their own fields.

The First Baptists sold their farms
and moved to town. Their children
found jobs in cities and moved away.
The retirees go to church on Sunday,
watch reruns of *Leave It to Beaver*
weekdays, and avoid the national news.

If the First Baptists had read
their founder's *Key* to Narragansett,
would they have tried to learn Spanish?
Would they vote for those who want
to send their neighbors back to Sonora?

Pat Sturm reads, writes, gardens, and rescues animals in Weatherford, Oklahoma. She lives on four acres with her husband and particularly enjoys her association with Wednesday's Poets, who meet every other Monday.

Out of the Dust

Woody Guthrie took sides.
The Dust Bowl blew him
out of Oklahoma and he
started writin' songs, drawin'
a clear line between
us guys and them guys.
He even wrote a song about
Preacher Casey, wrote a gun
into Casey's hand and
let him avenge a woman
shot dead by a sheriff.

Woody Guthrie left a wife and kids,
strummed his way
to California along Route 66,
drew hatred from the Californians,
but adoration from migrant Okies.
He gave voice to those outsiders,
housed under cardboard or tin sheds
prayin' to feed their families
with labor in western fields.

Woody Guthrie wrote songs
about bein' bound for Glory,
and danged if he didn't make it.
Today we sing his praises
like he was a saint or somethin',

but nobody could be surprised
to find him floatin' on a cloud,
restringin' his guitar, and
flickin' dust off his halo.

Strength of Character

"Them damned ol' ornge tigerlilies"
(thanks, Dad) give Herculean
effort. Smaller than usual,
lasting not quite as long, paler

than the audacious tangerine
of the past, they punctuate borders,
twist in the wind, remind us
that common is constant.

Spring did not burst forth this year.
Farmers cut skinny wheat.
Many specialty plants succumbed
to last winter's dry freezes.

Official records will proclaim 2011
"worse than the dust bowl."
Lucky for me, common orange tigerlilies
don't care.

Patricia Goodrich is a poet and visual artist. She has received Pennsylvania Fellowships in Poetry/Creative Nonfiction and was nominated for Pushcart Prizes in poetry and fiction. *How the Moose Got To Be* (2012), *Red Mud* (2009) and *Verda's House* (2010) are Goodrich's most recent books of poems. Her poetry has been translated into Chinese, Lithuanian and Romanian. Originally from northern Michigan, she resides in Bucks County, Pennsylvania.

Mosser Street

Mosser Street stretched for just one block---
Main Street tugging one end,
a plywood factory with fields and ponds behind,
the other---but that block of 1920's built houses held
moms and dads and grandparents and forty-some boys
and a handful of girls. I was one of those girls.

We weren't on the wrong side of the tracks,
but train whistles did mark time a block away,
and hobos slept in a gully behind our homeplate.
At one end we dragged home crates
from behind Willis's Grocery to make go-carts.
At the other we climbed trees, and boys bb-gunned frogs
and occasionally each other, and I learned to run
from dragonflies whose needle bodies were known
to stitch lips together.

One streetlamp lit the night
for Hide-n-Seek and Kick-the-Can.
Larry's backyard had the best sledding hill,
and when One-Arm Chris died, the new family
flooded his raspberry patch to make a skating rink
where the whole neighborhood was invited.
Our house had the first TV and the first divorce.

Family Business

White bread, butter and brown sugar
sandwiches. Not poor, like next door where
Veronica spread oleo, white as school paste,
from a tin for her runny-nosed brothers,
the youngest soggy in sagging cotton.
But we all watched our mothers sign
names on backs of credit slips
at Willis's corner store,
slips curled like snakes in the bottom
of the cash drawer until Friday's pay or,
wintertime, whatever alphabetical day
fathers stood in unemployment lines.
If a week slipped by without the balance
paid, we kids were sent with a grocery list.
And, rarely, though often enough to be
a dreaded possibility, instead of groceries
to take back home, Bessie gave us
a rootbeer barrel and a note, saying
No more credit until the bill is paid.
I never saw our dads sign a white register tape.
They reached into back pockets for wallets
and dollar bills, then emptied front pockets
every night, change sliding into cracks
of reclining chairs or tossed
into top dresser drawers, change
collected by wives and children,
change for the grocery store.

Small Change

A miniature brown bean pot, tucked
on the left-hand side of the highest
cupboard shelf. A pot of gold,
but no rainbow paved the way.
I leapt on burning coals each time
I stole pennies my mother hoarded there
to buy bread and milk between Friday pays.

I'd rather write about
my father's drinking at Frank's
Sportsman's Bar those paycheck nights,
not coming home until supper congealed
on the stove. Why Mother kept on
cooking, I'll never know unless
to feed my father's guilt.

Or about how almost poor we were,
but if my big brother or I hadn't touched
the jar, its change would have lasted
till week's end. I would tell you
about almost anything except
how I lied, swore it wasn't me
who emptied the pot.

How I stood by silent
and didn't save Bobby
from my father's razor strap.

Richard Dixon, retired Special Education teacher in Oklahoma City, currently works part-time at a municipal tennis complex stringing racquets, running tournaments and waiting on customers. During the state championships, he can be found at his executive position of changing out trash barrels in his trusty golf cart. Besides playing tennis, he enjoys writing, reading, movies and his grandchildren.

Birthday Card To Woody

Happy birthday, Woody. A hundred years is a long time. Here in Oklahoma we have an annual festival in your hometown with poetry and plenty of music, and now that you're officially centennial things are happening all over the place, and on a big scale. You wrote about such simple issues; now they're more complicated. Yet with changes upon changes they are more or less the same. We still have privatizing, deregulating monsters of greed who possess no compunction against continuously upping the ante to further fatten their coffers - - expert fear mongers who attempt to control through false statements that hit at the heart of insecurity, wage war on unions to further disappear the middle class, who in turn have no time to properly pay attention cause they're too busy looking for a job or trying to hold down the two or three they do have in an effort to get out from under that heavy-handed, usurious home mortgage or financing princely college tuition costs with a pauper's wage.

Yes, Woody, this generation also has a troubadour of the working class (Dylan, you may remember, quickly moved on from protest). Bruce has been writing songs about social issues for three decades now. He's been a strong influence, but not enough to even make a dent in this plutocratic juggernaut, government-by-corporation behemoth that's been building up (with short breaks) since Eisenhower warned us a half-century ago. He has a new record out that is his strongest language yet against this current culture of income inequality and climate-change denial in our rapidly deteriorating environment, against hypocrites who hide behind religion to stomp on individual rights and try to tell a woman she has no control over her own body. He's joined by some new tribunes, Woody, four true-hearted musicians who have released a brand-new batch of your songs, their music to your words.

This spirit, Woody, helped spawn an "occupy" city movement by one-percenters in public parks who were sneered at, spat on and avoided like they were diseased, by the same people who were responsible for bringing this country to the brink of financial ruin, than have the gall to turn around and scream panic that our first African-American president has had to further the debt in an attempt, successful so far, to keep this country out of an abyss from which there would be no return, to finally break the stranglehold of unemployment, and deal with all the other flotsam and jetsam left over from their eight-year party of corruption, incompetence and decidedly dire decisions. Obama also saved General Motors and killed bin Laden - - that's a re-election right there! These other people, though, are despicable, and they've all but taken over - - but I will continue to follow my conscience, be as active as I can in the battle and try, morally, to keep my head above the fray. In other words, Woody, I will try to keep following the example you helped set.

Richard Levine lives in Brooklyn, where he writes poetry and song lyrics . . . and sings. He has published several chap books of poetry and won numerous prizes and much recognition for his work.

Desert Wind

The Taliban forbids people
to own songbirds. They would
have Afghans know only
the craggy warbling-moan
of jagged mountain winds
and the raspy grit and drone
of desert sand blowing red
into the black-eyed poppy.

But if wearing niqabs does
not erase faces nor blind
caged eyes, can forbidding
force silence the songs
the world sings or still
the heart for having wings?

Huck Finn in the 21st-Century

Sometimes I like to think there are Jackson Islands that spring up wherever decent fugitives need an escape from the righteously wrong.

It's a comfort to think that, and to think that like Jim and me, there are those who don't subscribe to be so *sivilized,* who find it a comfort to think and live aloft, gliding the undammed currents of people in peaceful pursuits, abiding down the unpolluted rivers of history and precedent.

Sometimes I like to think like a field a farmer's let go free, to seed for a season, take it out of furrow and harness and let it breathe and be what the earth intended, free from the oppression of overseen rows that are hoed into where, when, how and what to grow. I like to think that people can live free, too, beyond the territories of profit, war, and bigotry that try to pull us up like weeds, out of jobs and homes and dreams, and post one-armed bandits to pen us in, hold us down and wake us up under the neon of the last *made in America* sign.

It's a comfort to think that you could drift free as a raft on the planet's one stream, beyond all the malls and flag-on-the-moon burdens, beyond the I-phone, Blackberry, twitter, Facebook, e-mails and direct tvs, beyond the account number identity thieves, beyond the strangling box-store chains, and telemarketing calls and mail, and drift all the way to the harbor of yourself, as if you always knew the way, and with one true friend find a sustainability that yields all you'll ever need.

Sometimes I like to think that for every huckster Tom in the skin of a warrantless politician, banker or other bloody-handed greed-king, there are a hundred like Jim and me, who touch wood and stone to mark everything in twain, and singing bird-loud of the unsung, cast out night deep trot lines and tie them off with every rapscallion's words and deeds to the ringed, trunk-tide and truth of a tree.

Robert Bell Burr grew up in New Jersey, attended Johns Hopkins University, ignored two induction notices then turned himself in, was re-classified (from 1A to 1Y) and set free, kicked around NYC for 10 years, became a typesetter, got a BA -1998, taught freshman composition for eleven years, now aged 67.

Long Sidewalks
(song-poem-lyrics related to W.G.'s "I ain't got no home...")

Just like walking long sidewalks
It's like riding out all night on a train
It's like wondering where you are, not knowing
It's like looking for a home in the rain.

Old crazy Willy, he cooed like a bird,
through the winter I heard him loud and clear.
One day he spoke to me these words so sad,
He said you won't see me around next year.

Just like walking long sidewalks
It's like riding out all night on a train
It's like wondering where you are, not knowing
It's like looking for a home in the rain.

Father Bill walks down the avenue
like a ghost ship that's headed out to sea.
He's asking me for change, I tell him I have none.
"That's OK [he said] don't take it personally."

Just like walking long sidewalks
It's like riding out all night on a train
It's like wondering where you are, not knowing
It's like looking for a home in the rain.

Where is the man who said he wrote a play?
Noble he told me was his name.
He drank two quarts a day, and all I could say
is no one no one is to blame.

Just like walking long sidewalks
It's like riding out all night on a train
It's like wondering where you are, not knowing
It's like looking for a home in the rain.

I saw a strange man awhile ago
come out of a doorway on both his feet.
He said "If I can't find a good place to rest,
watch me I'll rest here on the street."

Just like walking long sidewalks
It's like riding out all night on a train
It's like wondering where you are, not knowing
It's like looking for a home in the rain.

Rockford Johnson's poems appear in *Crosstimbers, 2005 Red Dirt Book Festival Anthology, Ain't Nobody Can Sing Like Me (Mongrel Empire Press, 2010), SugarMule.com # 35—Oklahoma Writing,* and *Travelin' Music: A Poetic Tribute to Woody Guthrie (Village Books Press, 2010).* His book: *All Things Flow* (Village Books Press, 2009).

Blue Dust on Divinity
(First of Four Poems on Remembered Plautdietsch Phrases}

Fe'lääje is the only word that really describes her,"
a woman of Mennonite heritage said of a friend whose
husband was slowly losing mind and muscle. The word
is a Plautdietsch, Mennonite Low German, word for
melancholy, for feeling blue.

Her words were coarse, her way abrasive,
like the grit paper she shimmied
on the legs of antique furniture. Working
at minimum wage, Linda had a place
in the rundown, half-painted, tin-roofed shop,
a place with five young divinity students,
single and married men who reveled
in debating the finials of conservative theology.

After a few cups of coffee, some days while she worked,
she danced a little to static-laced country songs
crackling out of the small dusty radio amid
screams of saw blades slicing wood, the pounding
of mallets, and one of the guys singing with Willie's
"blue eyes cryin' in the rain."

Jim stripped furniture in an acid bath
out back, laughed a lot, helped her sand,

134

and could get real serious about his dogma.
Gerald repaired arms, seats, legs, headboards,
when it seemed good told Linda God loved her
hoping to fix her aching, angry, blue-toned soul.

Hunter sanded too and stained the wood—preferred
classical not that country crap, his aged rural parents
had albums—and swore he wasn't gay.

Stan worked in the spray booth shooting new
finish on old wood—the final steps of renewal--
coughed a lot and claimed music heals the sinner.

Peter listened mostly as he worked but debated hard
when all five wrestled to defend deity with holy writ
against Linda's sharp, cross-grain swipes at the god
under whose direction they hoped to make a living.

Late most days, Linda dragged her slender,
nineteen year old body through the slam-back
shop door, her bra-less breasts draped
in loose, earth tone t-shirts above tight-fitted
Wrangler denims with wood stain accents,
or, on hot days sometimes, a simple shift dress,
her painted toes in leather buffalo sandals.

Red hair frizzled, wild and long, some days she was
hungover, sullen, some days mad and bitter. Linda
often slept, sandpaper in her hand paused
on a chair rung, forehead heavy on an arm.

At the creak of the spring-tethered door, triggered
by the boss or by Jim whispering "watch this,"
her hand would quick-start and her face lift to smile wryly
at old Mr. Smith or his henchwoman, Miss Barnes, or to fire
venom from her eyes at Jim and his relentless tease—

135

"Damn it, you goddamn preacher boy!"
She didn't work Saturdays, but the budding
prophets and cantors delivered furniture to noon,
went home to write sermons, plan hymns, help
a wife with groceries, play with a small child.

Sundays they preached, taught Sunday School,
led pious songs, thought of graduating and,
humbly of course, of glory. Mondays, having no class,
they worked all day in the restoration business.

That Monday morning, Linda slipped in very late
with a black eye, slept through the alerting door, was told
"Get out, don't come back!" She cried
slightly, briefly, raised herself off the bar stool, shook
the sawdust from her feet and walked toward the door.
"Linda, sorry," stumbled from Jim's mouth.
 "Go to hell! All of you just go to hell—
and take your weak little god with you!"

The door slammed shut.
The dust settled
on five speechless wannabes.

Going to Town Tomorrow
(Second of Four Poems on Remembered Plautdietsch
Phrases)

Ekj sie gone no ne Staut morje—*I am going to town
tomorrow.*

Strong black socks stretched up from inside
gray walking shoes, up from inside and over
the bottom of knee-stretched red red sweat pants.

Her black but graying, well shaped hair accents a painted
face, brushes the shoulders of a thin, shapely frame energetic
under the pure red sweat shirt—a superhero reflection.

She has been to town—Main Street, downtown—a small
purchase in the drugstore's gray plastic bag. She fidgets,
shuffles,
impatient for amber permission to cross the steady current

of young hands on petite steering wheels, of powerful trucks
curling lanes, bright sporty cars, dirty oil haulers,
farmers with hay spikes, and a school bus. She marches

to the light pole, demands long on the "walk" button for
a parting of the sea. The courthouse stands weighty
across the corner, city hall heavy next to her, law firms

on the other two points. She walks briskly across
the avenue to the side of town reputed dangerous,
small broken houses, hard working people making plans

to go to town tomorrow.

Ron Wallace, currently an adjunct professor of English at Southeastern Oklahoma State University is the author of five volumes of poetry. His first book *Native Son* was a Finalist in the 2007 Oklahoma Book Awards, and *Oklahoma Cantos* was a Finalist in the 2011 Awards. His newly released book is baseball themed and entitled *Hanging the Curveball*.

The Ghost of Okemah

Someone wake up Woody Guthrie,
tell him to grab his old guitar;
Oklahoma Hills are leaning hard to the right,
and there's wolves howling at the door;

Someone snuck in while the place was dark,
painted the whole damn state bright red,
and Jim Inhoff's authored up a bill
that forbids even skies from being blue.

Someone wake up Woody Guthrie.
We need a balladeer, a voice singing loud,
someone with a little bit of reason
who understands the working man.

This land is our land; he once said.
Then who shoved it so far off the track?
Who flung common sense, headlong out the gate,
opened up the locks and filled it full of hate?

Someone wake up Woody Guthrie.
He helped the little man stand up once upon a time,
pulled the big boy's boot right up off his throat
and leveled up the playing field.

Somewhere out there in the black of night,
the ghost of Okemah stirs before the storm,
strumming on his six string,
spitting nails and looking for the light.

Someone wake up Woody Guthrie.
        It's time to get back in this fight.

They Rise from Fading Grey Paper

They rise from fading grey paper
of a photograph
        so old
it can no longer hold them.

Dad on the right, Uncle Ira on the left
        time has eaten them;
from the knees down,
their legs, taken by years,
blend into the background dissolving
        in a blur of leaves and trees.

But their faces won't fade.
They wear Steinbeck smiles,
their dark hair curling from beneath their hats
        and jackets over bib overalls carry
eighty years into another century
where they appear to lift from the thirties' dirt
of Oklahoma or maybe Texas.

Chests and shoulders hold their heads high.
Unafraid of hard times
        or hard work

they look into the camera
grinning like Woody Guthrie
        as if they know
they will soon ascend from cotton fields
from the fruit trees,
from the stranglehold of slave labor wages
        overcome the fading photo,
and rise,
rise into perfect cloudless blue
        singing
about riding ponies in those Oklahoma hills
        where they were born.
Okies to the end.

Sally Rhoades hails from New York State's North Country where she grew up poor but fed. She has been writing poetry for over thirty years and performs at open mics. Both her mom and Dad were laborers from the depression era. She began to write their stories and her own.

My mother was a waitress

At Martin's when she was
Young and we were
Babies not even four
Or five. My mother

Was a waitress at
Martin's all day
Long. I wish I knew
her there how she delivered

The coleslaw setting it neat
On the side of the plate I
tipped my waitress over
Twenty percent. She said

Thank you & I realized
She has my mom to
Thank. My mom was
A waitress at Martin's

When she was young
She loved banana splits
& so when she got home
We'd find the dishes. She'd

Cut the banana &
We'd do the scooping &
Splashing and she'd
Place the cherry on top.

Battered, Hurt, little girl,

where are your spritely
curls?   Where, oh

where, are you   do you
live now   down

deep in the damp
Basement?   How

Harsh is your life
that feels the pain

all the time   even
when it rains   I feel

your pain   How much
terror can you take

nightmare   when you
wake   Little girl

with the fresh curls
Don't be afraid

The water is deep
But you must wade

142

There is no solace
In false pride

A child who sings

like a morning dove
will rest in between

Sing out the pain, the
hurt   the Battery

and let the Scowl of
a generation be heard

Sandra Soli, a regular contributor at WoodyFest events, received an Oklahoma Book Award, LSU's Eyster Poetry Prize, and two nominations for the Pushcart Prize for her poetry. Her work appeared recent or is forthcoming in Naugatuck Review, Ruminate, Parody, Tilt-a-Whirl, and Cross Timbers, among others. Sandy enjoys puns, and collaborative projects with artists in other disciplines. She is addicted to Downton Abbey.

Buchanan Street

Once I lived by the tracks.
Hobos would knock at the back
door, asking supper and chores.
Some shuffled their feet,
wouldn't speak.

All of us afraid.

For swept porch steps I'd trade
fried bread, beans, scraps off a ham
bone. When they were done
I'd hear "Thank you, Ma'am"
and they'd be gone.

All of us alone

Same Only Different: A Letter to Woody

The more things change, more
they stay the same. Politicians,
for example, have learned to Tweet.
Legislators snag lifelong salaries
and attractive assistants
Governors are the same, though
states go broke a little faster.

CEOs and bosses are the same.
Bankers and trustees still hide
assets in deep back pockets.
Board members, executive directors
and councilmen are the same,
fascinated with feasibility studies.
Complete this form, buy a license.

Specialists and consultants are the same
though insurance is questionable;
at times they amputate the wrong foot.
TV sponsors are family companies.
Spokesmodels smile on camera.
See. Our. Mouths. Move.

Bobblehead broadcasters offer
sound bites of news, where
things stay the same, doubtful.
And of course, the wars. Generals nod yes
because they want airplanes for their dogs.
Feds are the same, and we are often afraid.

Prophets know what is coming, as
they always did. Chairmen and chiefs,
chefs (and balances). Woody, all of them

still here – Plutocrats, weasels and snakes,
perverts, con men and profligates,
general sorry asses and corruptors.
The same. Same. Same.

This is the thing: we *remember* you.
Workers in cubicles and ditches,
fields and kitchens, on loading docks
and parking lots, ordinary sloggers
remember. We hear you, Woody,
plucking strings, singing us strong.

We have red dirt under our nails
like you. We live low to the ground
with fence mice, like you,
and spit in the dust on a dry day,
learning to speak louder. Different.

Sharon Edge Martin has been published in dozens of small press and commercial magazines and in Michael Bugeja's *The Art and Craft of Poetry*. Her chapbook, *No Sanctuary*, was published by Amelia Press. She writes a weekly column for *The Oklahoma Observer*.

Street Folk

If cleanliness is next to godliness
We're all going to hell
Try washing your clothes
Without soap or money
Wash your hair
Using restroom foam and no towel
Maintain your dignity
When people passing on the sidewalk
Veer away

You learn to spot your fellows
By those over-the-shoulder looks
On entering McDonalds
The way they shush their kids
Coming in the door
How long-timers
Try so hard to disappear
Into the background of ordinary
And, forgive me, by the smell

Privilege

Out here, roads aren't graded
Country lanes still iced over
A week after the blizzard, but
In the land of abundance, eat
Grapefruit for dessert, feed
Sparrows and squirrels, leave
Heat lamps burning for my chickens

In northern India, a cold spell
Kills dozens of street people
My chickens have better accommodations

I remember one hut, fence
As back wall, roadside as floor
In Mumbai, at night, drove past squatters
Around a sidewalk fire
In Surat, said no
To a dirty-faced child who mimed eating rice,
Gathered fingers to mouth

The guards at the jewelry store
Sent her away, and I bore only the burden
Of guilt as I purchased a gold bracelet
I keep locked away, gold
That could have sent her to school, changed
The future for her children and theirs

Brother, Love

Ransom told me about his first boyfriend
when he was twelve
He and Jody would walk through the cemetery
holding hands
and Ransom would come home smiling
But later, after he had time to think
he'd cry himself to sleep

He asked me, his big sister, if I thought he was crazy
to like boys "that way"
"No," I told him, "I like boys that way, too."

Jody and his parents left town
after someone carved an F on his forehead
F for fag

Ransom didn't do much hand holding after that
He didn't go out for sports
but he could sure talk cars
He started a lawn mower service
took engines apart
and pieced them together again
wore the grease under his fingernails
for protection

(Winner of Writer's Digest Prize, 2011)

Sylvia Riojas Vaughn, a Houston Poetry Fest 2011 Juried Poet, has had poems in *The Applicant, From Under the Bridges of America: Homeless Poetry Anthology, 2011*; *Texas Poetry Calendar*, Rio Grande Valley International Poetry Festival Anthology *Boundless, Illya's Honey, Red River Review, FORCES 2012*. She belongs to Dallas Poets Community.

Grandfather and the South Texas Mine

> *Another union organizer,*
> *Way over in that union burying ground.*
> —Woody Guthrie, *Union Burying Ground*

Grandfather escaped Mr. D's shotgun wielding goons
in the middle of the night. A knock on the door,
an urgent rush of words came in time to pile his wife,
children, brother and belongings on the truck.
They fled into the winter and uncertainty.
In the mining town, Grandfather tried to unionize,
agitating for better pay and working conditions.
Piercing rescue alarms sounded too often for Grandfather's
taste.
Families were jumpy despite dances,
movies, baseball games against farmers.
The children attended a one-room school,
eager for the daily delivery of milk and sweet rolls.
The men never handed wages to their wives on payday
with the kiss of satisfaction: Salary, credit at the company
store.
Grandfather settled in Laredo, worked for the railroad.
Coal dust's in my blood, the rumble of trains too.
And too many bosses exploit workers for my taste.

Not Nasal But Still Woody

Cuttin' that wheat, stackin' that hay
— Woody Guthrie, *Hard Travelin'*

And I've been hittin' some hard travelin', lord
The Kingston Trio sings harmony,
banjo, guitars blazing.
I began traveling at six weeks old.
Mother and I rode a bus from Texas to D. C.
By the time I spin Father's vinyl on the high-fi,
I've lived in three states and the Territory of Hawaii.
I'm ten.
I'm trying make about a dollar a day
Six years later, I begin to work.
Pour coffee at dawn, mop up after drunks.
Pack eggs, tote meals to the sick and dying.
Minimum wage for j-school not hard gamblin'.
Wound up reporting death in factories,
men killed in robberies,
heavy loads, worried minds
way down the road.

Stephanie Jordan is a farmer and chef, as well as an advocate for local food systems and accessibility to healthy food in poor and rural areas. She is the Ag issue chair for the state chapter of the Sierra Club and sells plants and produce at the Farmers' Market.

waiting for rain

in a hundred-year-drought
you learn not to hope
wishing just hurts too bad

knees bent to the earth
the withers of your faith
lie shriveled
in the dirt
once again

unconsciously accepting
your parched, hardpan destiny
you keep farming
because it's all you know
because it's what your father did
and his father
because civilization evolved
at the edge of a of husk of wheat

it's in your marrow
travels your genetic fingerprint
fires information
through neural pathways
under your skin

so you scrape the barren dust
and answer that ancient pull
sweat and toil
surely, there is nowhere to go
but up

fate's cruel fingers
touch your furrowed brow
once again
you mortgage the farm
sell your horses
sell your soul
for the bag of seed that
has to work this time
because there is no other place
for you to imagine yourself
in this world

you plow, sow, wait, pray
clouds gather
then pass

most days, you can no longer
meet your wife in the eye

the life you painted for her
a younger you, courting
convincing her to leave
the sanctuary of her sisters back north
to dream this land with you
the orchard you promised,
the rose hedges and spring lambs

instead you share dust storms
and threadbare reserve

she is worn down
parched in her own way, brittle

that she hasn't given up on you
hurts worse than drought
you can't even bring yourself
to absorb her tears

you feel her stare
her need
and find chores to do
hearing her break down
as the door clicks closed

eye to the horizon
you stand resolute
and wait

Steven Schroeder was born in Wichita Falls, Texas, and grew up northwest of Amarillo in Oldham County. From 2002-2009, after twenty years of teaching and peace work in Texas, Illinois, Indiana, Iowa, and Ohio, he taught philosophy, poetry, and peace studies at Shenzhen University in China. He teaches at the University of Chicago. His most recent poetry collection, *Turn*, was published in April 2012.

Woody,

You know it ain't no
machine. It ain't no machine.

It's the secret of a warm friend's
hand, the secret of a sea
of them,

a sea of ears that hear, of eyes
that see, of hands that clap,
of feet that dance,

of dreamers dreaming, dreams
we dream, and you
know why.

Speakers speak and preachers guess,
some say no and some say yes
and a lot of people preach

a ticket out of here. But you know
there's no earthly way
but to bow your head and stay
right here right now where

we stand. There's no place in this world
we'll belong when we're gone, so
we're just gonna do it while we're here.

Weather's gonna break, hell's gonna fly,
Clouds are gonna bust, rain's gonna cry.

All them fascists will still wonder why
we're not waiting for some sweet bye
and bye. We know it ain't no

machine coming. Nobodies nobody
knows, we know there ain't no ticket to be

had. We just say no. We just say now.
We stand. We remember.
We dream.

St. Louis, Waiting for the Train
St. Patrick's Day 2012

Sun rose on the emperor's mound
hours ago, the one they call "Monks" now
because some brothers who promised to say

only when necessary occupied it
centuries after the builders
had moved on.

Their children scattered as children do,
until nothing was left to tie them
to the place but stories
grandmothers tell.

Trappists should have known
an abandoned city when they saw one,
but they had in mind a place

to pray. That would be the city. I am thinking
of the backs that must have been broken
carrying all that earth, but not spirits.

Dig here for earth to make a high place
there but know what rises will fall.
And the walls. The walls.

What riffraff lived on the other side,
the side I'm on now -- corner of the National System

of Interstate and Defense Highways that might as well be
logs driven into the ground around the holy places
where the sun rises when the time is right,
covered with mud.

What goes up must come down, and I wonder now
who will walk softly on these ruins in a thousand years,
think them sacred, say how tragic they are gone --
what grandmothers will tell stories
to tie the children to them

Tony Mares comes from parents who belonged to labor unions, and he worked as a laborer to pay for college. He taught history and Spanish at Florida State University, University of North Texas, Colorado College and University of New Mexico. He has admired Woody Guthrie since childhood. His recent books are *Astonishing Light: Conversations I Never Had With Patrociño Barela*, University of New Mexico, 2010, and *Río Del Corazón, Voices From The American Land,* 2011.

---

remembering Woody

on old Route 66 I walk by
this elderly, white bearded man
slowly ambling along
wrapped in his filthy blanket

I wave a friendly "hello'
he responds with a look of pure
malice takes my measure
and spits we both go our separate ways

and I wonder what makes him
so sane what makes him see
my world modest as a small loaf of bread
so out of reach for him

I'm walking this same street
Woody walked in the '30's
this same grizzled wreck in his blanket
walked by Woody waved
his friendly 'hello' and the man
spat at him Woody being Woody
took no offense smiled and walked on

now eighty some years later
I can do no better than walk on
Woody at my side and smile
it's a long long fight
for this old fellow Woody says

don't give up now Woody says
we are all walking Route 66 again
and it's a mighty long road

The Factory of Loneliness
(thinking of Woody)

Long lines of Coca Cola
Were seen marching towards the border

The Big Mac Early Warning System
Had been overrun by rebel marshmallows

Shirts made in Bangladesh were ordered
To dig trenches along the polluted rivers

The news spread that The Factory of Loneliness
Was under assault. The Cables babbled on

About Communists and Anarchists poisoning
Citizens with messages of love and kindness

From on high the drones targeted free verse
And took out stacks of organic toilet paper

Inside the Factory of Loneliness machines
Without hearts marked the passage of time

With an eternal digital hum. After all,
It was The Factory of Loneliness

Under attack from all directions. To the South
A thin line of naked penguins waddled

up from the beaches. In the East
Freedom Fries surrendered to broccoli

The Factory of Loneliness was doomed
 No one, no one loved the Factory of Loneliness

Far to the West, salmon took back the Columbia,
 The Snake. The Colorado, the Rio Grande,

Were overrun by giggling trout
Meanwhile, down from the North

Came the winds of change bringing rain
Again to the man-made deserts of profit.

Inside the Factory of Loneliness machines
Without hearts would have sobbed,
had they feelings, to hear the long lines
Of us humans coming up from everywhere

Singing "this land is your land, this land
is my land." The Factory of Loneliness

Crumbled to the ground. Little children
Smiled again and played in the ruins

And that's the greatest thing
we have ever done.

What Would Woody Say

to a war against the poor in Afghanistan?
to a war against the poor in Iran?
to a war against the poor in Mexico?
to a war against the poor in America?

You say: there's no war against the poor.
Oh yeah? Ask the drone victim in Afghanistan.
Oh yeah? Ask the worker's widow in Iran.
Oh yeah? Ask the worker crossing the Rio Grande.

You say: Not in America. No war here.
Oh yeah? Why does the NRA control the Congress?
Oh yeah? Why does everyone carry a gun?
Oh yeah? Why do we fear the police?

Woody would say:
We need more guitars to kill fascists.
Woody would say:
We are all deportees.
Woody would say:
No peace as long as one person starves,
One person needs a job,
One person goes hungry.

Woody would say: Get off your butt.
This land is your land.
This land is my land.
Let's take it back.

Woody Guthrie at Raton Pass

Way up on Raton Pass
Woody stands and watches the world
Roll by. Along comes a Mercedes Benz
And Woody won't let it through
'til he waves a magic wand and turns
It into a Chevy, Now go on, he says.

Along comes a beat up Ford wheezing,
packed with phony protocols
Of the Elders of Zion. Thought you was
A VW with all them lying words, but at least
You ain't airtight, he says, and kicks it
Down a steep canyon where it burns.

A rusty yellow bus filled with kids
Comes grinding up the pass, the radiator
Hissing like a dragon. Then it dies.
Not so fast! Woody cries and he sees
The worried look of parents
And old folks inside. Can't make it

Says a whiskered grandpa. Yes we can
Says Woody. He rolls up his sleeves
Grabs that bus by its old bent fender
And pulls it up up up. Doesn't even
Taka a breath 'til the bus is safe over the pass.

I see him up there, old Woody, sometimes
Cisco too. They're hollering about
human rights, no more wars for capitalist
imperialists. They keep a lot of fat cats
off of Raton Pass, off of the best places
that belong to everyone, not just the rich.

Travis Blair lives near the University of Texas campus in Arlington, where he earned his degree in English Lit. For years he worked in the movie business before turning to poetry writing. He is author of *Train to Chihuahua*, and his poems appear in various literary journals.

Learning Life Lessons from Dad

As a kid, I spent my summers
working Dad's construction crews--
men who taped-and-bedded sheetrock,
textured ceilings and walls,
hard, hot work for an honest wage.

Dad paid me five dollars a day,
started me on an "idiot-stick,"
a sand-pole used to smooth rough edges
before texturers and painters came in.
I remember how my arms ached, my eyes
burned, my nose filled with sand dust,
but I slept like a rock every night.

Poncho, a migrant from Piedras Negras,
ran Dad's crews. He had three sons
who tagged along with him every day.
They earned a few dollars sweeping debris,
picking up nails which they put in cans,
sold back to my dad for pocket change.

Poncho's sons didn't speak English,
never bought lunch from a vending truck,
ate tortillas and beans with their father.
But in the 100-degree-heat of afternoons,
my dad bought popsicles to cool them.

He told me they sent their meager earnings
back home to Piedras Negras.

Some weekends Dad took me and Poncho's sons
to baseball games, bought us peanuts, cokes.
I remember he sat in the bleachers, a beer
in his hand, a grin on his face, watching us
have fun. Dad was a quiet man. He taught me
life's lessons without saying a word.

Yvonne Carpenter's poetry has appeared in literary journals and been published two volumes, *To Capture Fine Spirits* (Haystack Publishing), and *Barbed Wire and Paper Dolls* (Village Press). She and her husband raise cattle and wheat on a Custer County, Oklahoma farm.

Storm, 1939

Gathering all the available light
cottonwoods glowed white,
towering
over the shorter, darker brush.
In a veil of red dirt, the sun
masqueraded as a faint moon.

The black cloud came
from the west and south,
stopping traffic,
clogging lungs.

It was a Sunday in April, 1939, she said.
We had been to a motion picture in Elk City.
On the way home, the sun went out.
Traffic stopped.
We were stopped for hours.
That's the day Henry proposed to me

Beatitudes

Blessed is the heat that shatters the wheat,
cooks the petunias, blisters bare arms.

Blessed is the wind that torments the yard art,
pounds the windows, rolls up the roof.

Blessed is the dust that shimmers in the sunset,
cicadas that whine, ragweed that wilts.

Blessed is the catfish stranded in the dry creek,
car seats that scald, goat heads abloom.

Blessed in the horned toad scurrying like a leaf,
asphalt that melts, ants working at noon.

Blessed are drought, fire, and flood
humbling us with force immune to guns and charm.

Okies Then and Now

Atop a short mountain in the San Joaquin Valley,
we celebrated Uncle's ninetieth birthday.
Handed a photo for identification,
he looked past the children
to the car on which they posed.

That's a 1926 Essex. Dad bought it new.
Used it in the field. Kept jumping out of gear.
Transmission wasn't up to the work of plowing.
Traded for a '28 Dodge.
Fitted it out for camping.
Rented out the Oklahoma farm and worked the California
fruit harvest.

From another table, I heard,
They cut off our water and our peach orchard died.
Their green lawns were browning.
Told us not to worry, we would have water next year.
We platted the farm, sold it to a developer.
Moving to Saskatchewan where there is still room to farm.